Victorian Yorkshire

£1

By the same author

ILKLEY: A Visitor's Guide

Victorian Yorkshire

by
J.R. Thackrah

Dalesman Books
1979

The Dalesman Publishing Company Ltd.,
Clapham (via Lancaster), North Yorkshire.

First published 1979
© J.R. Thackrah 1979

ISBN: 0 85206 506 X

Printed in Great Britain by Galava Printing Co. Ltd.
Hallam Road, Nelson, Lancs.

Contents

Cover illustration of Saltaire Mill from an engraving by H. Warren.
Photographs on pages 33 - 40.

Preface

I HAVE spent some time making a study of Victorian Yorkshire —probably one of the richest periods in the county's history.

Few people, after reading local historical works, go out into the area and see the things about which they read. I hope, however, that after reading this book, the reader — and I am aiming primarily at one who is not an expert in the subject matter — will be sufficiently stimulated to visit for the first time, or revisit with fresh objectives in mind, the places both rural and urban that are mentioned. The historical sites that made Victorian Yorkshire one of the main foci of industrial, commercial and leisure interest in the nineteenth century well repay examination.

I thank many kind people who have provided help — in particular staff of Ilkley and Bradford Public Libraries and the Yorkshire Archaeological Society Library of Leeds, and my parents who have kindly encouraged me in the research required and ultimately read and typed the manuscript. There may well be differences of interpretation from those expressed by the authors of many books on this field of local history and I alone stand responsible for the comments and observations made in this book. If the work helps to stimulate interest in the history of Victorian Yorkshire I shall be content.

1.   Introduction

ONE OF the many achievements in Yorkshire resulting from the longest reign of any British sovereign was the transformation of society from the age of water and steam power to the onset of electricity. Cities grew prodigiously, housing covered many square miles, warehouses replaced elegant houses, factories were built without consideration to humanity or landscape, and with all this came prosperity to the manufacturers and the towns. Large country estates were being slowly dismantled into smaller units, and by the end of Victoria's reign the country mansion had passed its prime. The railway and iron and steel manufacture spread to the north and south of the county.

Agriculturally, a revolution occurred even though the climax of the first Agricultural Revolution had passed. In 1837 the only machinery was the windmill with no threshing/reaping machinery, no horse rakes. Ploughs were heavy and cumbersome, with no potato washers, elevators or chopping machines and butter making was in churns. By 1897, the transformation in agriculture was almost complete. There was an abundance of machinery, steam ploughs, and grain elevators. Good roads existed in all three Ridings, with railways and steam engines, horseless carriages and traffic on canals and rivers. Social movements of the Victorian era drew away people from the villages and changed the fabric of life.

The Industrial Revolution and its aftermath witnessed technical innovations unsurpassed plus huge economic, social and political changes. The county produced a rich crop of famous people who made their mark on many facets of life, from Delius to Kearton, Forster to Oastler. Yet the social life of the greater part of the population was rigorous, hard and quite unsophisticated by learning of any kind. Working conditions were harsh with little time for energy or leisure. The middle class did not dominate Yorkshire due to the predominant industrial areas to the south and west. Rural Yorkshire was changing and contracting. What happened in Yorkshire in the nineteenth century was partly controlled by the challenge of the political and social revolution, but also powerfully affected by the increase of wealth, fashion and the flux of opinions.

During the initial 25 years of Victoria's reign there was development of motion and factories driven by water power — perhaps the most outstanding achievement in Yorkshire. Alum works were centred on Guisborough until that industry died along with Whitby jet (recently revived) in the 1850s. In the field of iron manufacture a startling growth occurred at Middlesbrough by the river Tees on the edge of the Cleveland ironstone belt: from one house in 1829 to 25,000 by 1861. The docks opened a year later. At that time the iron ore bed yielded 50,000 tons an acre with 30% iron. Much of the iron went to the south of the county for use in the embryonic steel industry situated on the banks of the Don at Sheffield, where in 1855 the Atlas Steel Works was opened at Brightside and in 1862 a rolling mill for armourplate was built. Other mills such as Bessemer, Cammell, Vickers, Rogers, Mappin and Firth were opened later.

Textiles were an important facet of early Victorian life and by 1860 Yorkshire figured highly in the £17 million average annual value of woollen goods manufactured in Britain. Each town in the West Riding was a centre for a different facet of the industry: Leeds for woollens and worsteds; the Colne valley for cheap woollens; Huddersfield for fine woollens; Bradford for worsted and women's dress materials; Batley, Spenborough and Dewsbury for mungo and shoddy (mungo was clothing shreds already manufactured and shoddy the shreds of soft materials, while flock was scraps from machines); Wakefield, Bingley and Keighley were yarn centres; and Halifax catered for worsted yarn plus alpaca and mohair manufacture. While the textile and engineering industries were thriving the Enclosure Acts (operative since 1760) were busy absorbing seven million acres until then cultivated by peasants or the poverty stricken rural population. This was completed in 1862/7. Much land was used for the production of food which could be transported rapidly on the railways between Rotherham and Sheffield (1838), Normanton, York and Darlington (1841), York and Scarborough (1845), Bradford and Leeds (1846), Hull and Bridlington (1848), and Leeds to Wakefield and Goole (1848).

Yorkshire played an important role in the national economy in both agriculture and industry during the important years of growth and change after 1850. Although a period of prosperity then existed, there was a patchier performance during the final quarter of the century, coinciding with growing competition from other European countries and the decline of iron and steel manufacture, coal mining and ship building — the old style industries.

Coinciding with the momentum of the Industrial Revolution was the obvious establishment of the main centres of population (York, Leeds, Sheffield, Hull and Middlesbrough), in their own way built haphazardly and at speed to keep pace with the ever expanding industries which were part of the vast economic explosion — the Industrial Revolution. Social and living conditions deteriorated rapidly, being sacrificed to promote the new industrial growth that brought great affluence to a few and indescribable poverty to many. Cottage property with cellar dwellings was the most popular type of housing thrown up during this period because it was cheap and more houses per acre could be crammed together. Sanitation and general hygiene were non-existent; neither was there any proper drainage or piped water system. The reason for the high mortality rate, and suffering that accompanied it, lay in the ghastly housing and working conditions.

Harsh conditions at work for old and young alike left little time or energy for leisure and it was not until the turn of the century that the city matured as a balanced social unit, or that leisure and learning took their rightful places alongside industry and production, but by that time the Victorian era had passed. Many opted out of such city life for service careers in the army or navy. The county's most famous regiment — the West Yorks — fought in the Indian Munity, the New Zealand Maori Wars in the 1860s and in the Boer War. It was garrisoned also in India, West Africa and Gibraltar.

Amidst the Industrial Revolution trauma there was a high noon of Victorianism from 1850 to 1875 — a lull, a centre of indifference and interlude of relative quiescence and indecision between the political activity of the first half of the century and even more drastic changes that marked its close. The rapid growth of the Industrial Revolution, affected by the power of capital and enhancing the power of capital as well as emphasising its dangers and defects, was likely to develop in Britain a classic pattern of class conflict — conflict between capital and labour. Nevertheless, although the characteristic processes of the nineteenth century — the urbanisation, the mechanisation, the development of factories — had begun, they had not penetrated as deeply into the life of the community as perhaps one is apt to think. The Industrial Revolution was a benevolent movement, designed by far sighted philanthropists for the good of humanity.

Despite many thoughts to the contrary, the England of mid century resembled the cruder pre industrial, pre democratic, resolutely unreformed England of the 18th century more closely than we have been pleased to imagine. Yet Victorian England was a community in which powerful forces both creative and discordant were at work. The Victorian era had opened with the spectacle of the destructive power of the Luddites, who rioted against the use of machinery; and the militant political activities of the Chartists. Under the surface, powerful forces—the increase of population, the Industrial Revolution, the religious revival and increase of literacy and personal self consciousness—never ceased to do their work.

Townscape of Victorian Yorkshire—a study of Keighley by F.J. Mitchell.

Unlike Georgian times, the personal power of the monarch had to a great extent evaporated and a real party system had come into existence. Yet in 1850, the political system was still to a remarkable degree the plaything of the nobility and gentry and in particular of hereditary owners of great estates. There was little that the labourer could do to improve his lot. He was not in a position to found an effective trade union and was out of the way of political agitation. Not until the 1867 Reform Act did the system break — from then the increase in wealth, increase in self consciousness and confidence in the section of the working class created a new social group. Coinciding with such changes was the rise of trade unions and the changing contraction of rural England.

Victorian England was no doubt to a large extent the creation of the political and industrial revolutions of the nineteenth century. Two definite currents of opinion affected men's minds throughout the century and made Victorian England a scene of politico-social revolution — the movement from oligarchy or aristocracy towards democracy and the revival of religion.

The Victorian employer ruled with a rod of iron. He and the parson epitomised the characteristics of West Yorkshire. The mill and the chapel dominated every village — the first because of its immensity and severity, the second because of its size (often not so much smaller than the mill) and also because of its symbolisation of a lofty position. Both mills and chapels were like black stone coffins—the former in the valleys and the latter dominating the hill tops. Both mill and chapel were utilitarian, despite Graeco-Roman excrescences. Sundays were preserved for religion — perhaps as relief from the drudgery of the mill. At the start of the Victorian period, dissenters were under disabilities, while the Church of England was revived in Yorkshire after Bishop Hook's appointment at Leeds in 1837.

The Victorian employer was no doubt religious and was more influential in the woollen industry than in mining as many works of literature — Dickens, Brontë — would have us believe. It is definite, however, that mechanisation came earlier into the Lancashire cotton industry than to the Yorkshire woollen industry. Yet before long this industry and the related worsted ones at Huddersfield, Bradford and Halifax were organised on a factory basis, using steam powered machinery. This mechanisation coincided with the closing down of small water-powered mills in the Dales. One can gauge the importance of the woollen industry to Yorkshire's economy by a study of the 1851 census (30th March) which was the first one to record in detail the full names, age, head of each household, sex and relation of all members and working conditions of the population plus the parish and county where born, the number of houses, family sizes and the occupations of the persons.

The spread of this large and varied industry was just one example of the social movements of the Industrial Revolution which drew away the people and changed the fabric of life. Thus for such cities as Leeds, Bradford and Sheffield, the nineteenth century saw the most extensive expansion for they were 'boom' towns of the Industrial Revolution. The growth in cities was accompanied by a growing thrift and help attitude. Building Societies were developed, Post Office Savings Banks were created in 1838, the Bradford Improved Commercial Society developed as did the Second and Third Equitable Societies in 1851 and 1854. It was a period of great wealth for the city, but also of much poverty for many of the workers who flocked to its growing industries. By 1838—the start of the Victorian era—there were over a hundred woollen mills employing 10,000 workers in Leeds, and from contemporary reports Leeds had assumed by that time 'the characteristic face of a West Riding town, with a forest of mill chimneys sprouting thickly about the town'. Apart from textiles the early Victorian age witnessed a rise in the number of workers in other new industries, especially the engineering trades.

The early part of the nineteenth century was a very harsh period and has probably been made to seem harsher than Britain of earlier centuries because we know more about it. Yet even in mid century forces of order were able when concentrated to deal with ease, and so with humanity, with any major disorder. The working class, however, would soon change such a situation for they were moving into a position in which they could compete as a class for their position in society, soberly and effectively, and not as a body of picturesque rebels to be pitifully defeated.

Aristocratic power in the country was one of the important factors making Victorian England. It had presented itself at first in the formidable shape of old noble and landowning interest, which for a long period dominated the political and social life of the country. The process of history began to shake that domination, though large fragments remained. Meanwhile there had been forming a new type of aristocracy, a new caste, more extensive, more adaptable, less open to attacks of economic change or of discriminatory taxation, and that aristocracy remained in full vigour when Victorian England came to its end.

The aristocracy certainly took second place to the radical, reforming zeal of the Bradford citizenry with Wood's accounts of the brutal exploitation of women and children in the mills, Oastler's social work and the creation by Keir Hardie of the Independent Labour Party.

What happened to England in the nineteenth century was partly controlled by conscious human reason, as in this matter of the challenge of the political and social revolution which ran through the whole century and gave logic and direction to its history. It was also powerfully affected by such blind forces as the increase of wealth and also other factors less easy to trace, by fashion, by the flux and reflux of opinions which seemed tangential to the main argument of history, by emotional appeal and by snobbery.

Victorians had to realise that until man learnt to deal with the problem of unemployment and grant the working man a minimum wage there was bound to be hardship. Attempts to legislate improved living conditions in cities were defeated by private industries. Change came so slowly that there was little time for social adjustment and townspeople contained the character and features of countrymen.

Yet soon the Industrial Revolution had stamped its characteristics on the Yorkshire scene—machine and not handicraft industries which were driven by power predominated. Operating units were relatively large and there was a growth in the settlement unit. Between 1830 and 1850 the basis of the modern rail system was created and by 1844 the state enforced technical standards of instruction. Not until 1875 was there a modern system of public health, although by that date there had been a 30% increase in real wages. A change in working class standards was reflected in the growth of working class political and industrial organisations. Strikes became more common among textile workers, printers and file grinders. In the 1842 summer, heat caused problems—mills were idle, poverty and unemployment rife, riots and strikes occurred, the military alerted and prisons overflowed.

The rapid growth of towns and the impact of the Industrial Revolution changed the face of Yorkshire from what it had been in past centuries. Rotherham was typical of the growth in a Victorian town; the Town Hall 1826, workhouse 1839, Corn Exchange 1842, public cemetery 1842, public hospital 1869 and Market Hall 1880. In the traditional industry, textiles, England north and south both wanted woollens for armies and civilians, so there was plenty of work for Yorkshire.

Yorkshire in Victorian times remained an idea, not a place. The attributes for which Yorkshire and Yorkshiremen will be remembered were the products of Victorian England. All that was heavy and arduous in Victorian England flourished in the county— coal in deep seams, blooms and billets of hot steel under steam hammers, with wool being spun and woven in cold sheds. The freedoms of justice, the vote, the ability to pursue one's own course, worship and the emphasis on one's heritage, sport, open air activities and education were all prevalent. The hands of nature and hands of men have given Yorkshire a particular quality which may be indefinable, but which is evident in the landscape, buildings and craftmanship.

The Victorians found themselves with cities where the poor were housed worse than animals—with great tracts of industrial land scattered haphazardly with factories, and slums where there was no drainage or water. Often there were no schools, policing and little or no system of local government. The towns were left by the Victorians in today's pattern with the public offices, sewerage, hospitals, schools and water. To the early Victorians, famine and revolution threatened the whole nation, while to later Victorians, England was so secure that nought could shake it.

From 1870 to 1901, coal was already being displaced by oil and steam by gas and electricity, wool and cotton by artificial fibres and the horse by the motor car. This laid the way in the post Victorian era for the coming of the aeroplane, radio communications, atomic energy and space travel. The Industrial Revolution had changed Yorkshire and harnessed new forms of energy to the processes of manufacture. In Yorkshire, collieries, steel works, mills and factories existed side by side in increasing numbers and in harmony, helped by the railway revolution. Thus it was in transport that the revolution in scale went furthest of all. Cities in consequence of their growth were largely Victorian, with the era of villa buildings in towns and cities remaining so until large scale twentieth century changes in road development and slum clearance and tower blocks.

2. Agricultural and Industrial Revolutions

THE ERA from 1750 to 1850 transformed the West Riding of Yorkshire into one of the world's workshops—an Elizabethan age of industry and new discoveries. The onset of Victoria's reign witnessed the culmination of the Agricultural Revolution and the rapid climax of the Industrial Revolution—both events overlapping for a short time.

The Industrial Revolution naturally had an enormous effect on the economic history of Yorkshire whose most important interests were bound up with mining and manufacturing rather than agriculture. The substitution of machinery for hand labour necessitated a change from the domestic to the factory system. This led to a concentration of population in towns, a move accelerated by the rapid growth of parliamentary enclosures. Commencing at the end of the century the general use of telephones and electricity both as a motive and lighting power rendered the return of the factory to country districts feasible.

Outside the five West Riding towns—Leeds, Halifax, Huddersfield, Bradford and Wakefield—farming was the principal occupation. Dales farms which blended with the surroundings were still being built in profusion. The Yorkshire Show was started soon after the Royal Agricultural Society had been founded in 1838. Farmers generally were anti Corn Law. New crops (roots and clover) were already in existence plus new animal breeds and husbandry and new implements and techniques. In many farming settlements a degree of self sufficiency existed in manufactured clothing with many home farm looms; for instance in the rural area round Saddleworth, merchants were engaged in a busy trade with the United States via Liverpool. Indeed until 1855 the major piece work weavers were outside the factories.

The Industrial Revolution, as epitomised in Yorkshire by the coal and textile industries, created a new type of workman, the mechanic whose instruction and idealistic social superiority would tend to improve the skill and practice of classes of men conducive to the prosperity of the rising manufacturing towns. The West Riding textile area was a world of its own; a sombre, hilly world whose 'frontier towns' were Leeds, Bradford, Halifax and

Huddersfield and a concentration of one general interest with great diversity of application. It was clear that the Industrial Revolution in Yorkshire gave wider opportunities of material advancement and intellectual culture to the people. Large scale production necessitated wider markets, while unsatisfactory conditions of factory labour led to trade unionism and factory legislation. There was a new era from 1863 in iron and steel production with the creation of Bessemer's converter followed by Siemen's open hearth furnaces, plus the growth of a great engineering industry bringing the steam engine to the acme of development.

In mid century, despite such developments in industry and agriculture, there was little that the labourer could do to improve his position. As noted in the previous chapter, he was unable to found an effective trade union and was out of the way of political agitation. To indulge in incendiarism, which had in the past been one way of expressing his grievance, was merely to commit a brutal and useless crime, especially so soon after the Chartist failure.

Nineteenth century developments in the West Riding occurred on coal measures: an area stretching from Leeds south to the Derbyshire border and from the Pennines to the Magnesian limestone near Tadcaster. Coal and iron bearing rocks, running water, stone, clay and wood were used in the new mills and factories. There was an immense and rapid growth in industrial cities: for instance the population of Leeds grew from 172,023 in 1851 to 428,572 in 1901. Cities such as Leeds in consequence of growth were largely Victorian and remained so until the changes of this century. Smaller country or market towns were subjected to less rapid and extensive change and decay while villages were dusty and deserted. Warehouses and office buildings dominated the centres of such cities as Leeds and Bradford.

Yet, even in industry there were slow reactions. For instance, for woollen manufacturers only 5,000 power looms were operating in 1835 and until 1855 the major piece work weavers were outside the factories. Despite this fact, from 1840 to 1850 the exports of mixed wool and cotton fabrics made dramatic increases. Industry and the centres of population served to exacerbate problems inherent for centuries as towns and cities grew too rapidly, outstripping the capacities of sanitation and water supply. Local government bodies appeared inadequate. By the nineteenth century half trained surveyors and unpaid constables were an anachronism. Sanitary inspectors and ministries of health were unheard of and the teeming multitudes of poor had not enough houses, no amenities and no concept of the dangers of pollution. Not until the last year of Victoria's reign were the Esholt sewage works opened, with 53 acres of filter beds, the wonder of the world.

From 1850, Bradford like many Victorian towns in Yorkshire and elsewhere went through a period of rapid building which stamped it as a 'Victorian town'. In 1855 the City Council erected the first of the statues to eminent men. This was Sir Robert Peel, who was the founder of the British police force and abolished the Corn Laws. Bradford's first park opened in 1863 and was named after him. Forster, the educationalist, died in Bradford on 5 April 1886 and the city honoured him with a statue and named the central Forster Square after him. The town Forster represented from the 1890s paid its greatest tribute to his memory by the zeal it showed for education and the reputation gained as a local authority. Margaret Macmillan, the educationalist, was working in Bradford from 1893 and did much pioneer work in the education of children of all classes.

Mill hours were a shocking indictment of the Victorian factory system—resulting in low education. Liz Bentley worked in a Leeds flax mill at the age of six from 5 a.m. to 9 p.m, and in a tailoring factory the owner's three daughters worked from 3 a.m. to 10 p.m, with only 30 to 40 minutes for dinner. Mill hours were the same all over the county.

By the time Victorian mill development had reached its zenith, the effects of the Industrial Revolution were being felt throughout Yorkshire. Agriculture was on a rapid decline, commencing with an agricultural depression at the start of the last quarter of the century. It began with those sections which were dependent on the price of corn. Little doubt existed that disasters to agriculture affected the structure of politics. The stability of the mid Victorian period had in part rested on the balance of prosperity between industry and agriculture. After 1874 that balance was permanently upset, for what happened to agriculture was more serious and more lasting in its results than any setback suffered by commerce or industry, and the disastrous conditions in the countryside helped to shake aristocratic control of the county constituencies with results that were evident in the 1880 and 1885 general elections.

The repeal of the Corn Laws in 1846, much to the annoyance of Yorkshire people, had been seen as a measure to ruin agriculture, especially as in the 1830s and 1840s there had been progress and improvement. Better cultivation and the use of manures and fertilisers, e.g. bone meal, phosphates, and guano, helped reaping, threshing and sowing and the harvests were improving. Vast areas of northern and western Yorkshire were grazed by cattle and sheep and large plantations were created from mid century, such as the Duke of Norfolk's 1,500 acres near Sheffield. Drained, manured land gave 36 bushels of wheat per acre, while 22 bushels were obtained from undrained manured land. Flax, teazle and dyers woad were found on the marsh lands around Cawood. Potatoes were grown on the warp lands near Goole and chicory and mustard were also common crops.

Much of this land brought under cultivation was worked by Irish labourers who came to England in 1846 following the failure of the Irish potato crop. Most of the Irish belonged to the lower labouring class, the others being the upper (squires) and middle (tenants) classes. Good relations, however, existed among workers of different social classes. Many of the Irish immigrants also worked in the mills of the West Riding which were coming into their heyday as the influence of agriculture was declining. As a result of the Irish and others flocking to urban areas from the countryside, cities expanded. The Irish people posed a principal threat to the Yorkshire combers' position, for combing had been practised in Ireland and was not hard to learn. By 1851, the year of the Great Exhibition, machine combing was a certainty. Many Irish lived in Leeds, a 'boom town' of the Industrial Revolution which witnessed both a great wealth and opulence but also much poverty for many workers who flocked to its growing industries.

In Leeds, the city's expansion was the most rapid; its population growth the greatest in Yorkshire; its buildings the most splendid and its area very extensive. It grew from a country town of two square miles, built round a bridge over the river Aire, to a city covering 59 square miles of the mid West Riding. Mills in city areas by the end of the century mostly possessed electric light, the county's first electric light plant being built at St John's Colliery, Normanton, in 1883. The city also housed one of the most dominant factory buildings in the whole country—Marshall Mill, erected between 1838 and 1840 in Egyptian style with cast iron columns, brick ceilings and glass domes. A Town Hall was opened by Queen Victoria in 1858, a new Corn Exchange in 1868, a White Cloth Hall in the same year and a produce and cattle market. The Queen on her visit described Leeds as a 'stirring and thriving seat of English industry embellished by an edifice not inferior to those stately places which still attest to the ancient opulence of commercial centres in Italy and Flanders'.

By 1860, the heyday of Benjamin Gott's clothing processes had passed. The ready made clothing trade which rapidly established itself in Leeds in the mid nineteenth century demanded cheaper quality cloth than that produced by Gott. It was cloth which made Leeds famous, just as worsteds did for Bradford and weaving for Halifax, Huddersfield, Dewsbury and Batley. In 1856, John Barran, a southerner, had settled in Leeds and had soon installed two or three sewing machines in a small factory for making wholesale clothing. Two years later, having seen a bandsaw cutting wood veneer, he thought of substituting a knife for the saw and with the aid of engineering firms made a bandknife for cutting thicknesses of cloth. Thus the clothing trade started, helped by the railways, the proliferation of engineering firms and an exodus of Jews fleeing Russian pogroms to settle in Leeds. The development of customer cloth in the Victorian era culminated in 1900 when Montague

Burton borrowed £100 to buy a shop in Sheffield.

The slow change to power looms to quicken production was due more to resistance on the part of labour than to the absence of perception of opportunity by mill masters. Small scale cloth makers came together in a partial integration system and jointly carried out cleaning, dyeing, carding, spinning and finishing, whilst warp and weft were worked up on looms of industrial makers. The process of wool conversion into broadcloth was done both inside and outside the mills. Huddersfield, where Sir John Marsden was the ground landlord for the growing industrial town, concentrated along with Dewsbury (where shoddy fever was common) on the production of short stapled wool, while Halifax and Bradford concentrated on long stapled wool.

By 1870 power triumphed, but declining factors after that time reduced overseas demand, whilst increasing the popularity of worsteds which did not become well established in Leeds and left Bradford in a dominant position in the trade. Before 1850 the merchanting of cloths was already moving to Bradford, while the Leeds Cloth Halls' historical markets and social centres of the merchant class disappeared as the nineteenth century waned. Rapid development of woollen cloth occurred in centres to the south of Leeds, so that the town lost its central situation in the cloth trade. Employment fell from 14,894 males and females in 1851 to 11,722 in 1901. Dyeing firms declined from 63 in 1863 to 22 by 1913. Nevertheless, from 1875 to 1914 there was a high annual turnover of woollen textiles—around £7 million. By 1870 Leeds was the first centre in Britain for leather output. Both Leeds and Bradford had participated extensively in every important branch of clothing manufacture. By 1896 an observer could write:-

> Leeds is a vast place. When one enters the city from either station huge warehouses, large shops, big public houses and signs of active business meet one's view. Leeds is a miniature London and Boar Lane and Briggate are nearly as busy as London.

Leeds had advantages when the depression came in 1875. In an important period for the British manufacturing industry, trends differed somewhat from national ones. In a considerable period of falling prices, slower exports and adverse terms of trade which began in 1875, new industries in Leeds quickly filled gaps left by older industries which were on the decline, or were disappearing, e.g. wholesale clothing which grew as flax manufacturing diminished. This factor, plus the acceptance of technologies on the part of established and thriving industries, ensured a relative buoyancy of the economy of Leeds and its comparative prosperity in the 'Great Depression' period. Though Leeds suffered severely in all the short term depressions, there was no long term decline in the level of manufacturing activity in the town, nor the rapid expansion of routes and traffic. Its developed factory system would have been impossible if means of transport had not improved. Leeds Co-operative Society was 'one of the largest on earth', as one observer noted.

On the outskirts of Leeds, industry thrived such as machine tool and steam plough manufacture and from 1876 copper and engine works were established. At Kirkstall Forge, castings and wrought ironware were made for many industries in the area including equipment for coal mines. By 1874 there were 119 collieries in the Leeds area producing 3,150,933 tons, yet even this impressive figure could not compare with Barnsley where 55 collieries produced 3,646,109 tons of coal.

Vast industrial developments occurred on the West Riding coal measures, of which Leeds was at the northern end. In Keighley, for example, iron founders and machine makers were being added to the staple worsted spinners and manufacturers. The town also was a centre for textile engineering. To the south of Leeds, Wakefield was mainly an agricultural centre in the reign of Victoria, when other towns were meeting the growing needs of industries, and therefore the architecture was not as ugly as elsewhere.

Nevertheless, not all industrial development was confined to the West Riding. Alum works were centred around Guisborough until that industry died in the mid 1860s, while to the east on the coast at Whitby the jet industry thrived for some years. In 1873, 1,500 people were employed at workshops in the town and the trade realised £90,000. It was not until 1850 that a real bonanza occurred when, as mentioned in chapter one, ironstone was found at Eston Nab in the lower Cleveland bed of iron ore yielding 50,000 tons an acre, with 30% iron. Within a year 200,000 tons had been dug out, primarily for the manufacture of iron rails, and by 1856 this had risen to between 10,000 and 12,000 tons a week. There were six furnaces at Eston and four at Middlesbrough. The heyday was from 1875 to 1913, with the peak production for the Cleveland mines reaching 6¾ million tons in 1883. Smelting was carried out by Bolckow and Vaughan. Much was distributed at home, such as iron rails, and overseas via the port at Middlesbrough. In addition salt was discovered at Port Clarence and production increased from 3,134 tons in 1882 to 236,671 tons in 1889.

Lead ore or galena was mined to the west of Middlesbrough. After the depression in lead mining at the start of Victoria's reign, attempts were made in 1850 to revive the industry and partial success was achieved. Machinery was introduced for crushing, riddling and washing ore, driving smelt mill bellows and pumping out water accumulations. All this was expensive and increased production costs. Then in 1870 there was the increase in imports of lead from Italy and Spain, so Dales lead mining became uneconomic. The Grinton mines partly closed in 1880. Further south at Cononley, 15,000 tons of lead ore had been raised by 1882, where the deeper workings were up to seven feet wide. Near Pateley Bridge, in 1838, lead mines had an output of 2,000 tons. Investments by lead merchants were less important than in Derbyshire. Lime was also worked in the Dales, including Swaledale, but its heyday had passed by 1850. Perhaps surprisingly in Swaledale there were also a number of small collieries working coal in the Yoredale series. Stone was quarried in the Dales, but had finished by 1870.

While many of the Dales folk were engaged in lead mining or farming, back on the coast many inhabitants were making a living out of fishing. In Hull, fishing replaced whaling as the main activity—whalers having declined from 53 ships in 1819 to three by 1854. The industry was replaced by steam powered seed crushers—over 70 by 1870—used for oil extraction, with cattle cake manufacture, paint industries, flour milling and woodworking as offshoots.

Furnaces and cranes, harbours and docks, smoke and grime came with a rush and Victorians loved it. Yet as the ports and cities grew, great rivalry was developed between them. In Bradford, St. George's Hall was completed in 1852-3 and stood for the city's bold pretensions to commercial primacy in the West Riding. To Leeds this was intolerable and was countered with the opening of the Town Hall in 1858. Yet, in spite of the rivalry, no town could boast overall about its working conditions—industrial towns were grimy and no thought was given to the demolition of insanitary or old properties. Little relief could be obtained in terms of holidays; factory and shop workers had one half day's holiday per week until the Bank Holiday Acts in the 1870s gave relief from stress for workers in the city.

Sheffield did not need to indulge in such rivalry in view of its own prestigious production of specialised iron and steel. In 1860, Sir Henry Bessemer was attracted like Huntsman by the possibilities of Sheffield and established works for the production of mild all purpose steel by his new process which was not cheap by virtue of it not being mass produced. Through such developments the city increased in population almost threefold from 135,000 in 1851 to 350,000 by 1893. In 1865, one of any steel works in the city was capable of turning out every four hours a mass of cast steel. By 1867, for example, three-quarters of the plates of the new British ironclads were made at the Atlas works. The engineering industry in the city rested on the tradition of the 'little masters' or home workers who always retained a rough independence. The hiring of power was an old story in the area while the Sheffield of armament firms was rising amid the old Sheffield of cutlers. The Provincial Typographical Association, founded in 1849, had its first headquarters in Sheffield, a town rich in small, locally minded trade clubs. During the nineteenth century the steel industry was

22

transformed from craft workshops to a mammoth industry, while between Sheffield and Doncaster there were 37 forges and furnaces.

Agricultural and industrial needs were interdependent, especially in the valleys. Calder Valley was such a place. It prospered in the 1850s and little farmsteads on the hillsides and hilltops flourished to provide food for the population in the valleys. In the cotton and worsted mills built by hillside streams, young children were used predominantly for labouring. Weaving was the last major process to leave the home. The clothier's house and weaver's cottage were the pivot of the domestic system and places to which warp and weft work were brought. Hand loom weaving in the home remained the rule in the linen industry until the 1840s, especially in the Nidderdale area. As late as 1897, Walton's of Knaresborough described themselves as 'linen manufacturers by hand power'. Yet in the Dales, small water powered mills which helped the weavers were closed down between 1850 and 1900.

Mills were becoming larger; for instance in 1836, 140 cotton mills employed 10,000 persons in the West Riding, but by 1846 this latter figure had increased and mills generally were being extended. At this time worsted spinning was coming into its own with demand exceeding supply. Closer ties resulted between cotton and woollen manufacturers. Yet the absence of cotton during the American Civil War caused an exaggerated temporary demand for wool. Worsted yarn exports had a value of £637,305 and 1,971,492 pieces of woollen and worsted stuffs were exported. In 1894 at Low Mills, Addingham, there were 55 handcutters of velvet to cope with exports.

By the latter date the tradition of families in the same mill generation after generation was still strong. Most workers lived within walking distance of the mill, in terrace houses, many built before the 1840s. In the 1890s they cost between £30 and £100 and were put up by speculative builders and mill owners or individuals who built a row and lived in one. Many who worked in mills were children. Out of 4,651 children working in worsted mills whose ages ranged from nine to thirteen years, 4,185 were in West Yorkshire, and in the thirteen to eighteen age group, 11,951 out of 14,023 worked in the West Riding. In Leeds, as the noise and smoke increased, there was an exodus from the centre and even by the turn of the century houses had become offices.

As a result of increased urbanisation the communal preparation and production of food grew in importance in Yorkshire, centred on Leeds and Bradford. A cattle market was opened in North Street, Leeds, in 1855 and a new Corn Exchange in Call Lane in 1868. Market stalls were banned from Briggate in 1857 and a covered market built in Kirkgate. By 1875 the city had 130 cooperative societies catering for corn milling, boot manufacturing, tailoring and building.

With increasing housing and industrial development, mill chimneys presented a study in themselves. John Marshall opened his new flax mill in 1840, with a mill chimney disguised as Cleopatra's Needle, just as Titus Salt in the Aire Valley built a chimney at his mill, in the model village, designed as an Italian campanile. Wages in mills such as these often totalled £600 a week and between 1,200 to 1,500 people were employed. Wool sorters earned £1. 6s. 3d. (£1.31) to £1 10s. (£1.50); combers 14s 9d.(72p) to £1 6s. 6d. (£1.32); spinners 1s. 6d. (8p) to 2s. (10p); reelers 8s. 5d. (42p) to 13s. 9d. (67p) and bunchers 7s. 6d. (36p) to 8s. (40p). Wage differentials between 1837 and 1901 alone epitomised the changes in Victorian England.

The growth in wages, and the increasing use of large varieties of machinery in the production of a wider range of industrial goods and services, characterised the changes that had occurred throughout Yorkshire during the whole of Victoria's reign.

3.

Victorian Politics —Central and Local

LIBERALISM dominated central and local politics throughout the country and especially in Yorkshire. Reform of political administration made great strides from 1800 to 1900. Prior to 1832, reform had been slow. It was not until 1885, however, that any real reform took place—48 years after Victoria had come to the throne. Until 1882 the county had 30 to 37 parliamentary seats. Yorkshire from 1885 was represented in parliament by 52 members, half representing single member county divisions and the other half, twelve cities and boroughs. Such steps had been made easier by the passage of the 1867 Reform Act which enfranchised many new voters in the boroughs and more in the counties than are usually credited to it. In many boroughs the new voters were working men and from 1885 they included agricultural labourers.

Thus, from 1860 to 1880 the political structure of the county changed giving new significance and new possibilities to the type of agitation in which Dissenters engaged. A major cause of the change was no doubt the effect of social developments in the mid years of the century. In a large number of constituencies, the classes who had been content with the leadership of a large oligarchy in electoral matters had become sufficiently independent not to be content with a subordinate position any longer. Any electoral intimidation between the classes was brought to a close by the 1872 Ballot Act. In Leeds the city's MPs grew from one in 1832 to five by 1881. The 1888 County Councils Act gave rise to modern local self government in rural England, while in 1894 urban, rural, district and parish councils were formed.

The increase in the electorate and the machinery of local government coincided with the flourishing of trade unions among miners, textile workers, glass bottle makers, mechanics and workers in many less important industries. They became vociferous in 1875 at the start of the great agricultural depression predicted in 1846 when much land acreage was out of cultivation. Yet in a way their fears were unfounded as the depression cleared the out of date landlord and the hopelessly retrograde farmer. Some of these farmers were members of Arch's Union—yet this was the cause of greater disagreement between landlords and tenants. Landowners sympathised with unions or at least did not wish to antagonise men who it now seemed clear would at some time or other have the Parliamentary vote—this was eventually granted in 1864.

Continuous political agitation commenced at an early stage of the Victorian era in Yorkshire. The Plug Riots of 1842, for instance, were a reaction against economic hardship and started at Stalybridge. Perhaps surprisingly, Chartism had no unity or clear policy in Yorkshire apart from 'the Jones' attitude for a separate Church and State, the restoration of Church property, a voluntary system of education, the abolition of capital punishment; and a new Poor Law, Laws of Primogeniture and Entail, the repeal of Game Laws, direct taxation, a small propriety system and free trade. The Chartist movement did not survive, however, to see governments provide help for the benefit of the later Victorian populace. There were good transport facilities in all three Ridings plus sanitation, water supply, better housing, rights for the poor and the vote. Central government also introduced two other measures which affected Yorkshire: the compulsory keeping of parish registers from 1835 and the comprehensive census in 1851. Local government's areas of responsibility included the Poor Law, highways, burials, sanitation and schools. In 1839 a new Poor Law had been established—all persons were assessed for rates, and workhourses were built for districts of twenty or thirty parishes. As for workhouse inmates, the law laid down that sexes and ages were to be separated, with free medical attention and food.

In mid century, as already noted, there had been an interlude of relative quiescence and indecision between the political activities of the first half of the century and the even more drastic changes that marked its close. At the start of the Victorian era, Yorkshire was allocated 37 MPs and 25,000 voters, while at the end of the century the franchise had been greatly extended and the number of MPs nearly doubled. The 1867/8 Reform Act is a convenient year for historians to say that the old system had begun to break with the gradual extension of power to the working classes.

The government prior to the 1860s had nevertheless been concerned at the plight of the working classes. Unsatisfactory conditions of factory labour led to trade unionism and factory legislation. The 1844 Factory Act meant that no child could work before he was eight, and then only for six hours a day, while the 1850 Act stated that factories were to open only between 6 a.m. and 6 p.m. with 1½ hours for lunch. This marked the abandonment of laissez faire in regard to factory work. Shortly before the second Act a Central Board of Health was created to cut down the administration of sick people as a result of the rapid increase in industrialisation. The Act gave representation of Rotten Boroughs of Aldborough, Boroughbridge and Hedon and gave members to larger towns—Leeds, Bradford, Sheffield and Halifax. The increasingly rapid strides in industry meant that the 1871 Trade Union Act legalised unions for all purposes, while registration was not compulsory. Until that time, when a trade union collapsed, men were forced to get help from Poor Law Guardians. The JPs in Yorkshire had to see that such measures were implemented—they met in Quarter Session until 1888.

Municipal Corporation Acts of 1837 and 1840 revised charters of major towns from Richmond, Hull, Leeds, Doncaster, Pontefract, Ripon and York, to Wakefield, Bradford, Halifax and Huddersfield. Chartists had been concerned with the reform of central government. If every man had a Parliamentary vote all wrongs could be righted. They also put forward many demands for reform as the old fashioned system of local government was no longer suitable, even for villages. The various governments of the day had to take account of such demands for reform. Yorkshire towns were given the right to manage their own affairs such as water supply, police, street lighting, health and education, and to implement these measures councils were formed in Sheffield in 1843, Bradford 1847 and Middlesbrough 1853.

These later developments had been part of the Chartist demands dating back to the 1840s, which also included the vote at 21, the use of the secret ballot, abolition of property qualifications for MPs, the payment of MPs, equal electoral districts and annual parliaments. The Chartists had threatened that if Parliament did not grant their charter, they would bring the country to a halt by a long strike. Meetings led to threats and disorder in Barnsley and Sheffield. After the failure of riots in 1840 in Bradford and Sheffield they lost their way and were without a national movement. Yet health improvements were obtained plus better treatment for paupers. Chartists collected money (the National Rent), while many sat in a Chartist's Parliament (The Convention). In Lancashire and Yorkshire, Chartism assumed the character of an insurrection. Pikes were manufactured, an armed force organised and military training given. The government of the day countered by banning meetings or breaking them up by force if Chartists persisted in holding them and bringing ring leaders to trial. The penalties were heavy even for boiler tappers and plug drawers. Fergus O'Connor was sentenced to death and eighteen others to transportation in absentia. Leeds remained the headquarters of the 'Northern Star' until 1844, when it moved to the south. In Barnsley the Chartist Joseph Crabtree said that 'if demands were not granted, he would light a fire in Yorkshire that would not soon be put out, so England would be a heap of smoking ruins'.

The question of pauperism was one issue forced to the front of central and local government views during the Victorian period due to general conditions. Pauperism, the result of sheer improvidence, was caused by two factors: ignorance among working classes with reference to social virtues, and the ease with which ratepayers' pockets could be dipped into by the rate collector. Nonconformists at this time were in the political arena as a distinct party, and were appalled by the growth in paupers. As a result an anti State-Church Conference was held with meetings of pastors and flocks in both Yorkshire and Lancashire, but their influence in elections was weak —even in alliance with Chartists they were often defeated by combinations of Liberals and Protectionists and Liberals and Peelites. A major step in halting the exploitation of child labour as well as easing the lot of the hard worked labourer was John Fielden's introduction of the eight hour day in the West Riding, as a result of the Ten Hours Bill.

By the late nineteenth century, elected councils governed the whole of Yorkshire yet JPs meeting in Quarter Session still had a large say in government. Additionally, many of the magistrates were drawn from the gentry and clergy, especially in the West Riding. In the North Riding the first County Council elections in January 1889 returned unopposed gentry; Sir Henry Beresford-Pierce in Bedale, Earl Feversham at Helmsley, Sir William Worsley at Hovingham and Earl Zetland at Marske. Despite the predominance of gentry the Act gave modern, local self government in rural England. In Harrogate, Huddersfield and Keighley, local Parliament Acts created Improvement Commissioners for paving, lighting, cleansing, watching, regulating and town improvements.

Politics in the Victorian era were without doubt closely related to the rapid growth in industrialisation and the vast social changes that accompanied this revolution. Political matters moved a considerable way along the path from aristocracy to egalitarianism, and the lot of the ordinary man in the street was a great deal better in 1901 from what it had been in 1837.

4. Victorian Society

DURING the Victorian era, the social life of the population was limited by the conditions and type of work undertaken by many people—demanding, severe, treacherous and time consuming. Attitudes of employers to their workforce left much to be desired, and resulted in bitter strikes, for example in the coal industry. Dangerous working conditions had led to 26 miners being drowned in a flooded pit at Barnsley in 1838; hundreds were killed by firedamp; and in 1866 at Oaks Colliery over 360 men died. The first Inspector of Mines had not been appointed until 1850. Miners did not receive parliamentary representation until 1855 when, after one of the worst strikes on record, the first Yorkshire miners' MP, B. Rickard, was elected Liberal member for Normanton. By 1874, a miners' headquarters was established at Barnsley, followed in 1881 by the creation of a Yorkshire Miners' Association.

Many of these changes occurred in urban areas, for by 1870 the transformation from rural countryside to industrial society was complete. The Industrial Revolution drew away people and changed the fabric of life; villages decreased at the expense of towns and on a minor scale this resulted in what some saw as two related events—the decline of the village fair and the increase in drunkenness in the expanding towns. Drunken activities in a way resulted from the atrocious living and working conditions of the operatives which provoked reaction from the workers and humanitarian thinkers in the city: in Leeds for instance, rioting was a constant feature from the 1830s to the 1850s. Rioting was at its height at a time when the transformation from countryside to industrial town was complete in 1850; when groups of spinners and weavers moved closer together in the West Riding to work continuously in wool and make a living.

The optimistic hopes of the middle class and skilled workers set the tone of social life in late Victorian Yorkshire. Victorian complacency regarding squalor and poverty was rife, while the early Victorian employer worked like a slave and ruled like a slavemaster.

Religion was always strong in the Victorian period. At the start of the reign Dissenters were under disabilities, while the Church of

England rivived with a new diocese being created—Wakefield in 1888. Many of the religious people belonged to the middle classes, yet they were not to dominate Yorkshire even after the 1832 Reform Act. In the era of building in mid century, few churches and many chapels rose on every hand, with huge edifices being built by the wealthy. Except in the cities where a majority did not attend places of worship, all social life and popular activities centred around them. Famous preachers and ministers drew packed congregations. Attendance was often obligatory for employment, while men and women gave lifelong service and held simple beliefs. In 1850 a Roman Catholic organisation was set up followed by the Salvation Army. A year later, out of 983,423 attending places of worship in Yorkshire, two-thirds were in Dissenting chapels (i.e. 600,000). Chapel building increased apace starting in Yorkshire with the Hull Trinity House Chapel in 1843 and Mill Hill Chapel in Leeds in 1847, and by the end of Victoria's reign 'one Yorkshire city had a church for every 940 adults'. In another city, Leeds, besides Church of England places there were chapels as follows—seven Wesleyan Methodists, three New Connexion Methodists, four Associated Methodists, three Primitive Methodists, one Quaker, two Roman Catholic, eight Independent, one Baptist, one Unitarian, one Arian, one Inghamite, one Southcotarian, one Swedenborgian, one Jewish. These 35 chapels provided 30,596 seats. Many churches built prior to the Reformation were reconstructed in the Victorian era, e.g. Leeds and Ilkley Parish Churches.

As church and chapel became increasingly important in Victorian social life, so Sunday observance was taken seriously with chapel being the main focus of people's social lives, where they listened to earnest discourses. Yet at Sunday School children often fell asleep after mill labour. The relatively unsung virtues of Victorian churches, together with civic buildings, gave individuality to architecture. Not until 1880, however, were Englishmen who preferred to worship God 'chapel' fashion treated in every way equal to fellow Englishmen who preferred public worship in parish churches.

A strong link with religion throughout the Victorian period was the growth of education as many schools were church maintained. Many children in industry never had a chance to learn and, until the 10 Hour Bill and the 1844 Act, child slavery was exploited. Not until the end of the century was education put on a sound basis in Yorkshire by the pioneering work of the Bradford based Margaret Macmillan.

Few children received formal education compared with the vast number who acquired their learning at home, or through being apprenticed to learn a trade or craft. In Hull in 1838 a census of 4,735 ex scholars showed that 823 could not read a complete sentence and 1,870 could not write. In Leeds, 15,000 children went untaught. Sunday School was provided for 11,000 and less than 7,000 were in such rudimentary secular establishments as existed. Nevertheless, education of the poor was growing. By the 1880s Yorkshire's education system was socially stratified, a far cry from the situation 40 years earlier, when the Poor Law had allowed workhouses to cater for education. School boards were created throughout the county, such as at Leeds in 1871, and the opening of technical schools, in Huddersfield in 1850 and Bradford in 1880, coincided with a great surge in further education facilities. By 1886, 6,000 students attended Yorkshire Adult Schools of which 3,500 were in Sheffield, Hull and Leeds. Mechanics Institutes had been promoted and financed by manufacturers, clergy and professional men offering classes and lectures delivered by paid instructors and local enthusiasts, particularly in the sciences. Local authorities growing in status and confidence provided public amenities like museums, libraries and parks, and local papers made the working classes avid readers, e.g. 'Leeds Mercury', 'Leeds Intelligencer', 'Bradford Observer', 'Sheffield Times' and 'Sheffield Daily Telegraph'.

This impetus in education would not have been possible without the interest promoted in the county by the Education Act of 1870—initiated by the Bradford MP, William Forster, Minister of Education, who lived at Burley-in-Wharfedale. It was passed against the opposition of Anglicans and Nonconformists, and the resulting elementary education Act authorised the creation of undenominational school boards in educationally inferior districts.

The growth of religious and educational developments coincided with a rapid increase in population from 18 million for England and Wales in 1851 to 22 million by 1871, to 25 million by 1881, and to 36 million by 1901. From 1750 to 1850 tracts of countryside were transformed into industrial townships and in the next half century many of these towns became cities. Bradford's population rose from 80,000 in 1847 to 270,000 by 1900, while in 1847 the first charter of incorporation was realised. Not until the last decade of the Victorian era was there a decline in the number of people per inhabited house. This was especially the case in textile towns and was connected with the birth rate. The fall is exemplified in statistics, e.g. Bradford from 4.72 in 1891 to 3.2 by 1901.

The increase in population coincided with turbulent times for the industrial towns. In the 1840s there was distress among the labouring classes in Leeds due to the repeal of the Corn Laws and new machinery in the mills. The atrocious living and working conditions of the operatives resulted in industrial cruelty especially to children. The strap for instance had six nails in it at Mitchell's Worsted Mill in Keighley; while in the town there were 150 rickety children due to them being under-nourished. Such cruelty occurred at a time when many women and children did a man's job in the pits for 12 hours a day. In Leeds rioting was a feature in the late 1830s and during the 1840s. The Chartist, Fergus O'Connor, published his newspaper 'The Northern Star' in Leeds during the 1839 Chartist riots. The Chartists wished to make a revolution and were opposed by the Leaguers who asserted that a revolution had happened already. In view of this unrest at the start of Victoria's reign, the Chartists, whose works were disunified with no clear policy as to aims and methods, would have been horrified to realise that the optimistic hopes of the middle class and skilled workers set the tone of social life in late Victorian Yorkshire.

In the intervening period there appeared to be growing Victorian complacency over squalor and poverty. Little immediate notice was taken of the report of the Health of Towns Committee in 1840, which dwelt on insanitary conditions in Leeds streets—'all deficient in sewerage, unpaved, full of holes with deep channels formed by rain intersecting the roads, overflowing sewers and offensive drains'. Four years later Engels stated that 'Bradford was as dirty and uncomfortable as Leeds and similar to Huddersfield, Barnsley and Halifax'. In the same year a report stated that 'whole streets in Huddersfield were unpaved, sewered or drained, with rubbish rotting and fermenting'. Bradford was classed as the 'most filthy town in the north' at a time when the battle against squalor was costing only £3,000 and railway Bills £300 million. Ragged and bare-footed women and children were in abundance, often straight from the mines where until 1842 they carried coal to the surface. There was great wealth and squalid poverty. However, in Sheffield in 1864, the building of back to back houses was prohibited. Poverty was enhanced by the fact that in 1850, out of 500 mills in the West Riding, 300 to 400 used short time labour, many working on the 5,000 power looms, resulting in the absence of adequate wages. Poverty above all was noticeable in Leeds. For example, in the Boot and Shoe Yard, 340 persons lived in 57 rooms with an annual rent of £214 and only three out-offices or privies existed. Some 75 cartloads of excrement were removed from one eighth of an acre. Death rates, therefore, were high. In 1843 the average age of people dying was 24 in Sheffield, 21 in Leeds.

Thirteen out of every 17 inhabitants of Leeds belonged to the working class—including all the Irish workers and the 5,000 immigrants. Perhaps with the rapid growth in population, the surprising thing was not that people were badly housed but that they were housed at all. No wonder Dickens called Leeds 'a beastly place, one of the nastiest places I know'. This was especially true of the Leylands slum area where a large influx of poor immigrant Jews settled in the late nineteenth century, coming as refugees from

VICTORIAN TOWNSCAPES. Above: The view from Quebec Bridge, Keighley, in 1898. This area was in the heart of the town's Westgate slum. (Keighley Library).

Below: Penistone, where the impact of a steelworks erected in 1862 is all too evident. Terrace houses sprawl across hitherto open fields. (Biltcliffe Collection).

Many Victorian innovations set standards which long remained unsurpassed. This indoor market at Halifax, opened in 1895, was a far cry from stalls on draughty street corners. (Shibden Hall Museum).

Food at the door—although the standards of hygiene would not have amused a present-day public health inspector. This hot-peas' seller was travelling the streets of Keighley in the 1890s. (Keighley Library).

Men at work. A scene in Wm. Wright's Jet Manufactory, Haggersgate, Whitby, in 1890. The sombre blackness of jet appealed to Queen Victoria, and thus became a fashionable form of jewellery in the late 19th century. (The Sutcliffe Gallery).

Women at work. A group of traditionally-dressed fishermen's wives gather bait on the sands near Whitby about 1895. (The Sutcliffe Gallery).

THE AGE OF THE RAILWAY. Above: This engraving, c. 1841, by A.F. Tait graphically shows the impact on the upper Calder Valley of the Manchester & Leeds Railway, boldly cutting across the earlier canal and winding road near Hebden Bridge. (Science Museum).

Below: The railways enabled people to move about on a scale hitherto unknown. This 1849 scene shows race-day crowds arriving at Doncaster station. (Illustrated London News).

TURNPIKES AND TRAWLERS. Above: Hunter's Bar Toll House on the Sheffield to Chapel-en-le-Frith turnpike road, about 1884, showing the toll collector leaning against the side of the house. (Sheffield City Libraries).

Below: Steam paddle boats were in vogue throughout much of the Victorian era. The paddle trawler 'Star' is seen here at Scarborough, with several fishermen's carts on the sands in the background. (Scarborough Public Library).

VICTORIAN LEISURE. Above: An unusually silent moment for members of the Leeds Conversation Club, which met to discuss all subjects apart from politics and religion. This study was taken at Hellifield station during the club's 1882 excursion to the Catholic seminary at Stoneyhurst. (Leeds Central Library).

Below: Nigger minstrels were a popular form of entertainment: this particular show was put on at the Northgate Hospital, Pontefract, in 1900. (Pontefract Central Library).

HOLIDAY EXCURSION
TO
ESHTON
HALL.

The Committee of the KEIGHLEY MECHANICS' INSTITUTION, beg to announce that they have made arrangements for an Excursion to Eshton Hall, the Residence of MATTHEW WILSON. Esq.

On Whit-Monday, May 28th, 1849.
THE PARTY,
ACCOMPANIED BY THE KEIGHLEY BAND,

Will leave the Railway Station at half-past Twelve o'clock and proceed to Skipton, at which place a number of BOATS will be in readiness to convey them to Eshton Hall. After spending the Afternoon in visiting the

SPLENDID GROUNDS
&c. &c.

connected with that place, which, through the kindness of MR. WILSON, will be thrown open, the Party will return to Skipton, which place they will leave at Eight o'clock.

The Members and Friends, headed by the Band, will leave the Mechanics' Institution in Procession, at Twelve o'clock precisely.

Tickets to Eshton Hall and back;—

First Class, 2s. 6d. Second Class, 2s. Third Class, 1s. 6d.

May be had of Mr. Aked, Mr. Hudson, and Mr. Crabtree, Booksellers.

The Male and Female Classes will receive their Tickets at the Institution, on Thursday and Friday Evenings, from half-past Eight to half-past Nine.

Persons intending to join the Party, are requested to purchase their Tickets on or before Saturday Evening, that the Committee may make their arrangements accordingly.

J. L. CRABTREE, PRINTER, KEIGHLEY.

Whit Monday excursion, with band, in 1849. It made ingenious use of both railway and canal, and no doubt a 'right good do' was had by all. (F.W. Houghton).

VICTORIAN PERSONALITIES

Top, left: George Hudson, who created much of the county's railway system before financial malpractices brought his fall from power.

Top, right: Richard Kearton, born at Thwaite in Swaledale in 1862, w the first person to popularise natur history in Britain.

Left: Dan Leno, the famous 'Dam comedian, who won the 'Clog Dancing Championship of the World' at the Princess' Palace, Leeds, in 1880.

the Russian pogroms. Many found work in the tailoring industry, when at the turn of the century the ready-made clothing trade in Leeds was being rapidly developed. Leeds is a good example of a typical Victorian city in Yorkshire, to quote figures for the 1850s. There were 82,120 people (39,411 males and 42,709 females) composed of married 27,762, single 999, widows 2,990, lodgers 4,283, domestic 4,509, children 41,577; and 18,279 dwellings, of which 16,773 were English, 996 Irish, with 70 others and 440 unoccupied. There were 216 inns, 335 beerhouses, 98 brothels and two gambling houses. The passive population was 20,445 and the active 61,675, with 154 weekday schools and 20 factory schools.

Air was polluted by smoke from a thousand chimneys and in grimy streets children grew up who had never been to the country. Bradford, Leeds's neighbour, gives a good example of the mills' diversity—in 1847 it had 70,000 people, 80 worsted mills, 8 corn mills, 16 dyeworks, 280 stuff and woollen warehouses and 40 collieries. A balance could be created between the need for passable living conditions for workers and the necessity for industrial development. The prime example in Yorkshire of course was Saltaire, the model village created in 1853 on the banks of the river Aire by Sir Titus Salt. His commercial ability helped to establish Bradford as an international centre of worsted textiles. By 1850, he was the richest man in Bradford with five mills in operation plus outworkers and woolcombers. Above all he wished to alleviate suffering as the population increased at 5% a year from 43,000 in 1831 to 103,000 by 1871. At Thompson's Buildings near Shipley Beck, 95 people shared 23 apartments and 24 beds.

Salt's village gave workers the benefit of clean air and decent living conditions for a civilised urban life. Salt had foreseen the commercial value of alpaca cloth and built the biggest mill in Yorkshire between 1854 and 1872. Opposite the mill a Congregational Church was built. He then added 45 almshouses and 850 houses plus schools, a hospital, a library and bath-houses. His weaving shed held 1,200 looms and 30,000 yards of cloth and was considered the largest workroom in the world. Apart from alpaca, Orleans black cloth was a favourite product. Between 1851 and 1861 textile output doubled. Few people perhaps realised that prior to building Saltaire, Salt sought to make Knaresborough a manufacturing town, but his plans were vetoed by local authorities. Salt's view was that charity had no place and everything had to be paid for, even if for only a small sum.

Saltaire's good fortune contrasted sharply with the misery of Keighley and showed the gap between workers and aristocracy. By 1850 population growth here had outstripped the adequacies of sewerage, drainage, sanitation and water supply. An eye witness report stated that:

> Standing puddles were foul and offensive liquid matter seeped through the walls and cellars. Unventilated back to back houses close to the core mattress

and mangle manufacturing factories reeked bad air. Disgusting privies and soil pits, pig styes and manure heaps stank in yards and snickets.

In one, for instance, a single privy was shared by 29 houses — in others a ratio of 3 to 66 and 6 to 90. At Huddersfield, 20 lodgers were in four beds and at Halifax 19 lodgers had no beds. Rogues and tramps inhabited cellar floors—drinking, whoring, pilfering and fighting predominated. At Bradford excrement was in open channels; at Leeds rubbish was dumped into yards; and at Halifax effluvium was in damp and filthy holds.

Smallpox, dysentry, scarletina, measles, etc., exacted their toll; whooping cough, croup, influenza, diarrhoea, typhus and rheumatic fever killed; scores of people wilted and died of consumption, paralysis and asthma. At Leeds 28 persons had fever in seven houses, three of which were without beds, and the same ratio occurred next year with cholera. They were the unfortunates not to benefit from sanatoria or spas in Harrogate, Ilkley or the Dales. It was obvious in these conditions that crime such as vagrancy, over-crowding disturbances and prostitution were rife. At the other side of the county a report on Sheffield stated it was characterised by 'noise, smoke and dirt, with people in poor health'.

The sudden decision of the later Victorian politicians to improve public health in the 1870s showed a striking aspect of the mid Victorian era — the extreme briskness with which its prominent citizens could act when the opportunity or need arose. This attitude differed markedly from that of the early Victorians who were un-affected by the great poverty in Yorkshire — a starving population with mills on short time and bands of unemployed in the city sub-urbs pleading for charity. Partly as a result of such brisk action, in cities all over England there was a fall in the number of people per inhabited house, especially in textile towns where there was con-nection with the birth rate. In Bradford it dropped from 4.72 persons per house in 1891 to 4.36 by 1901; in Leeds from 4.71 to 4.53 and in Halifax from 4.45 to 4.21. Even in York in the 1890s, Rowntree stated that 28% of the population was below the poverty line.

Few of these classes of people went to church. Churchgoers were exclusively middle class. Workers stood on doorsteps or collected in groups until the time arrived when the service was over and public houses would open. To the workers religion was sombre and harsh, refusing to speak to their senses, imaginations or hearts. It was not surprising that it remained the patrimony and privilege of the well to do. Rightly or wrongly the poor man was treated as a pariah. Perhaps the workers were more in tune with the aims of the Leeds Redemption Society; that is man, instead of looking for scientific arrangements so skilfully contrived that the abundance of wealth produced would exceed his needs, had to learn to live contented without needing or desiring riches in wages. Yet the big gap did create tension and resulted in an unsatisfactory state of feelings which arose between employers and employees. In Yorkshire, for instance, the potters went on strike in 1866 and in 1877 the colliers and engineers agitated for more wages. A collier was only paid for the amount of coal he mined. A quarter of the country's miners were in Yorkshire and Lancashire. The highest daily wage was under 5s. (25p) and a weekly wage under £1. In 1883 a textile strike first introduced women to work in factories and led to trouble in textile mills—the first real problems since the woolcombers' strike during the Chartist era in 1843.

In spite of the privations and hardships there was a real community spirit. Each community supported its own schools, clubs, newspapers, shops, hawkers, village idiots and local dialect. As regards leisure time, life revolved round the chapel, church and home. Life for most people was provincial.

Victorian architecture was a striking aspect of the age. In the sandstone and coal above the millstone grit excellent stone was at hand for the surge in house building, mills, warehouses, town halls, offices and art galleries. There were two types of stone—ashlar, a grainless sandstone used in buildings, and Elland Flags for paving stones. It was the era of shops in which architecture found expression with the erection of precincts, arcades, markets and stores.

Visitors, both foreign and British, found Yorkshire towns not more agreeable than those on the Lancashire side of the hills, but smaller and easier to get out of with windy moors nearby. People from outside the county believed that Yorkshire townspeople retained longer, and more noticeably than men of the greater Lancashire towns, something of the character and features of country men. The development of social activities of the Victorian age brought all walks together as never before in what was, however, self-conscious mingling.

5. Transport

THE DEVELOPMENT of transport coincided with the Industrial Revolution and revitalised the whole aspect of life in the county as it affected advancement of trade and manufacture and leisure activities. Roads and railways were constructed with almost feverish activity and the population was rushed from the extremes of medievalism to modernism with breathtaking speed. Horse and wind power gave way to steam power almost overnight and the county, and indeed the country, was never to be the same again. Towards the end of the century came the development of the horseless carriage with its internal combustion engine, the forerunner of the modern motor car.

In 1840 there was a regular service of 13 stage-coaches a day between Leeds and Manchester, ten between Leeds and York and six between Leeds and London. The travellers must have been hardy individuals to put up with the bumping and jolting and bouncing of inadequately sprung vehicles on the potholed and rutted tracks that served as roads, on which it is said that on average one coach a day overturned. By the time the last Edinburgh-York mail coach ran in 1842 the railways were already threading their way across the county, and speeding up the transport of mail in the process.

The first passenger line wholly in the county, that between Leeds and Selby, had been opened three years before Victoria became queen, when the Marsh Lane tunnel had been 'the first in England to engulf an apprehensive trainload of citizenry', but the commencement of the new reign seemed to be the signal for a great surge forward in railway construction. The Rotherham-Sheffield link was inaugurated in 1838 and Leeds-York in 1839 and what followed might well be construed as a foreshadowing of present day complex timetables. The Leeds-Derby section commenced operations in 1840 and this opened direct communication between London and the industrial West Riding. In the same year the Leeds-Selby line was extended to Hull and the following year Normanton was linked to Manchester and York to Darlington. Bradford and Leeds were connected on the 30th June 1846 and this marked the opening of the first of the main Leeds stations, Wellington. Central followed in 1854 and New in 1869. Wellington was the successsor of the city's first station which was situated in Marsh Lane.

Progress so far had not required any exceptional engineering achievements but this deficiency was rectified with the construction of the line in 1848 between Harrogate and Church Fenton which linked the spa to London and the south of England. The track had to cross the Crimple Valley just outside the town and this was accomplished by the construction of a viaduct of 30 arches each of 52 ft. span, 130 ft. above the valley bottom and of a total length of 1,850 ft. The following year saw the fruition of two even more spectacular feats of engineering with the completion of the Leeds-Thirsk link and the trans Pennine route through the Woodhead tunnel to Manchester. The topographical nature of the county, which required innumerable river and valley crossings and the penetration of the Pennine range, proved not only expensive in financial terms but also in dimensions of human life and these two routes provide good examples of both cases. In the former instance the Wharfe was bridged by means of a viaduct between Arthington and Weeton, a structure of 21 arches each of 60 ft. span 90 ft. above the river with Westcoe Hill tunnel at the western end and Bramhope tunnel at the Arthington end, forming in the space of a mere half dozen miles a costly and spectacular enterprise. Bramhope tunnel is the eighth longest in Britain and cost the lives of 23 workmen whose memorial, in the form of a model of the tunnel, can be seen in Otley churchyard. The Sheffield-Manchester line was even more disastrous in the toll it took of the men employed on the construction of the Woodhead tunnel, during the course of which hundreds died as a result of outbreaks of cholera and the normal accidental hazards of tunneling operations. Tunnels naturally were a distinctive feature of trans-Pennine construction and that at Totley on the Sheffield-Manchester link and the one under Standedge on the Huddersfield-Manchester route are further evidence of the enterprise required to break through and overcome the difficulties of natural barriers.

It was, however, the Settle-Carlisle via Ribblehead route which provided the most formidable obstacles and proved to be one of the most expensive seetions of line in the country. It was constructed between 1870 and 1875 and was probably the last to be created by manual labour alone, hundreds of navvies living in shanty towns erected alongside the track as it progressed towards the highest point of any main line in England. The scenery encompasses Ribblesdale, Dentdale and Garsdale, the line passing Whernside and Ais Gill before dropping down to the Eden valley, beautiful and spectacular indeed but probably little appreciated by the men working often in the severest of weather conditions on the whole gamut of operations required in the building of a railway, from bridges and viaducts, to cuttings, embankments and tunnels and finally the laying of the tracks and signalling systems and the erection of the stations. Ribblehead viaduct and Blea Moor tunnel are the two most noteworthy structures of this magnificent engineering feat built across some of the finest scenery in the land.

Meanwhile lines of more modest proportions had progressed at considerable pace and opened up the county to all points of the compass. In 1845 York and Scarborough were linked and in 1848 Dewsbury was connected to Leeds and Goole to Wakefield followed by Skipton to Ingleton in 1849. Then came the York-Starbeck link which necessitated the crossisng of the Nidd at Knaresborough by means of a four-arch viaduct 300 ft. long and 90 ft. above the river. In this area the Pateley Bridge branch was also inaugurated, followed by the Bedale-Leyburn section in 1856. Surprisingly late, York and Doncaster were directly connected in 1871, though the South Yorkshire town had been the site of the Great Northern Railway workshops since 1853.

The opening of Richmond station on the 10th September 1848 demonstrated what a boom the coming of the railway, in this case connecting the town with the York-Edinburgh line, meant to one of the remoter parts of the county. This line enabled the inhabitants of Swaledale to have access to the Durham coalfield with its superior products compared with the coal extracted from opencast workings at Tan Hill, the only source available up to that time. However, due to the high cost of transport it was only the 'better off' that were able to afford the imported coal, the poorer classes still having to rely for some years to come on the inferior Tan Hill coal or on peat. The dale also benefited by the more readily available means of exporting the products of the lead mining industry.

The expansion of the railways gave impetus to the development of dormitory towns such as Harrogate, Ilkley, Otley and Wetherby and intervening villages, connecting them to the industrial West Riding. The middle class was quick to realise the benefit to be obtained from living in the country and yet still being within reasonable access of the factory or mill. It was not only the West Riding which witnessed the development of branch lines because they sprang up all over the North Riding linking such places as Pickering, Malton, Scarborough, Whitby, Saltburn and Redcar with the villages of Helmsley, Coxwold, Kirkbymoorside, Glaisdale, Danby, Egton, Robin Hood's Bay and Staithes. It is sobering to reflect that in something like a hundred years transportation progress and economic factors coupled with the 'Beeching axe' have seen the rise, decline and final elimination of so many of these branch lines to be succeeded in some instances with the revival of certain sections by groups of enthusiastic amateurs during the past few years.

The development and extension of the railways meant that the expansion of the ports was given added impetus and new routes

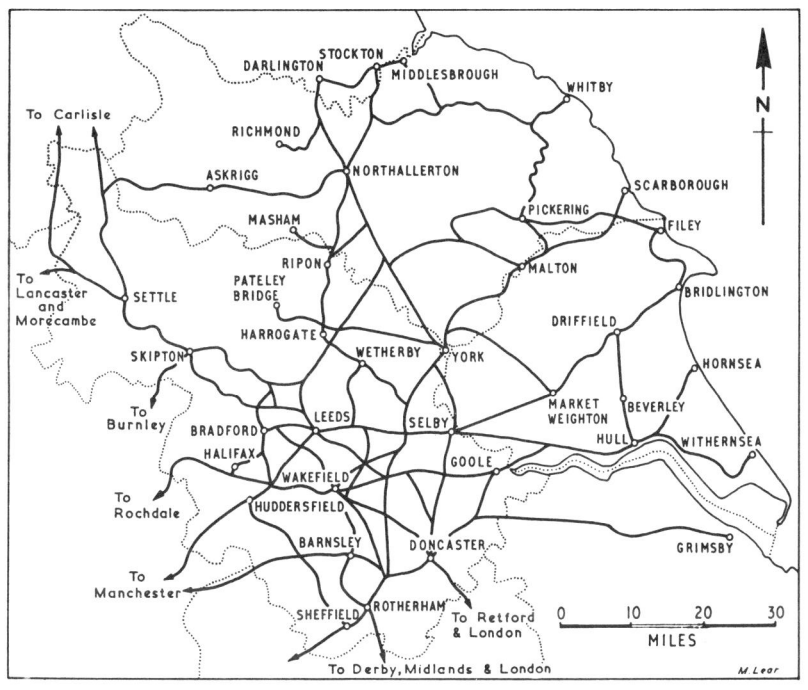

Railways of Yorkshire: an outline sketch.

across the world were initiated. Hull had three docks in 1830, and these were followed by Railway Dock in 1846, Victoria Dock in 1850, Albert Dock in 1869 and Wright, St Andrews and Alexandra Docks in 1880-85. In 1875 the service from Hull to New York commenced followed three years later by the Hamburg, Antwerp and Dunkirk services. In 1883 the route to Bombay was inaugurated by the Wilson Line. The port of Goole was opened in 1828 when a brig sailed for Hamburg. As late as 1840 it was nothing but a small village, yet it became in just a few years one of the country's chief river ports with extensive trade in such diverse commodities as champagne, timber, stone, iron, oil and general farm produce.

The rise of Middlesbrough was even more dramatic. The line from Darlington to Stockton was opened in 1825 for passenger traffic and extended in 1830 to Middlesbrough which was at that time a mere hamlet. In twelve years it became a port of considerable importance with docks on both banks of the Tees and a population of 5,463 in 1841 compared with 154 ten years earlier.

47

The port's development was due to the discovery of iron ore and limestone in the immediate surroundings, and it was these natural assets coupled with the railways and shipping interests which formed the nucleus of what, 150 years later, is one of the most heavily industrialised conurbations in the country. Middlesbrough was the first town in the country whose creation and development was a direct result of the new age of steam which itself flourished and progressed because the basic essentials of the iron and coal industries were close at hand.

The effect on the population of the coming of the railways must have been one of excitement and, to a certain degree, of bewilderment. The Settle-Carlisle railway brought cosmopolitan navvies and masons, engineers and dynamiters to bleak moors to accomplish the wonders of Blea Moor tunnel. Travel experience was broadened and enlarged to cover most of the country and, compared with stage-coach days, was cheap and fast; perhaps no other development before or since has done more to unify the nation and accelerate its prosperity consequent upon the rapid diffusion of information and movement of goods. In spite of sudden progress from the era of the stage-coach, travellers must have been hardy and intrepid souls, especially in the early years of the transposition. There were three classes of accommodation on the trains, those unfortunates choosing to travel second or third class often having to do so in open carriages exposed to the vagaries of the elements and the foul emissions from the engines. The more favoured ones travelling first class would at least have been under cover but the comfort must have been reminiscent of the old coaching days. All classes would have been subjected to the frightful din generated by the engines, which themselves were extremely unreliable and temperamental. Standards improved, though, and by the end of the century comfort and reliability had immeasurably changed for the better, and though speed had increased considerably the safety factor had also commendably advanced.

The coming of the railways had a profound affect on the Industrial Revolution enabling raw materials to be transported from the ports and other parts of the country to the manufacturing towns and cities of the West Riding, followed by the rapid dispersal of the manufactured products to all parts of the land and ultimately throughout the world. Socially it proved to have mixed blessings. Those who lived in the industrial areas were able to get away from it all from time to time by taking a train to the coast or country and thus becoming aware at reasonable cost of the beauties virtually on their doorsteps. On the other hand the railways were a principal factor in the depopulation of rural communities, the inhabitants of the villages being enticed to the towns and cities by the prospect of wealth and pleasure they could never hope to achieve otherwise. Whether their living conditions were improved in consequence is debatable.

The 18th century had been the age of canal transport but its usefulness was short lived because its industrial competitiveness rapidly diminished with the advent of the railways. By the end of Victoria's reign barge transport, picturesque though it was, had become an anachronism. Even the Leeds-Liverpool canal, of which 40 miles were in Yorkshire, was declining in importance.

Widespread though the railway network was, many rural communities were by-passed and still had to rely on coaches or waggonettes for inter-village transport or for travel to and from the nearby towns; and of course the carter and the farm wagons remained familiar sights in the countryside. The conditions of roads and their repair and maintenance remained something of a problem right through the reign. Indeed, two years before the queen succeeded, parishes had been responsible for non-turnpike roads by a Highways Act. Turnpikes were brought under the jurisdiction of local authorities in the 1860s and were finally abolished in 1871, though these authorities still had repair and maintenance responsibilities.

This system also applied in the towns and cities where transport for the masses was the horse-drawn bus, soon giving way to the similar powered tram running on rails which ensured a smoother journey for the passenger and an easier one for the horse. Leeds operated the first of these services in 1871 to the suburb of Headingley. Bradford's first route was from Darley Street along Manningham Lane to Lister Park; it commenced on the 2nd February 1882, each vehicle being drawn by a team of ten horses. The service was operated by a private company which leased the track from the Corporation. The same company started to use steam trams in 1884 but the noise was appalling and the speed excessive. The Bradford Daily Telegraph of 28th August, 1884, commenting on the fining of certain drivers by the local court, mentioned that: 'It was stated in evidence yesterday that the engine of one car was running at the rate of 12 miles an hour, a pace certainly too great to be tolerated in the town'. The first electric tram route opened in 1898 on Bolton Road, again operated by a private company. However, Leeds was the first city to have an overhead electric tramway system when in 1891 it opened the Sheepscar-Roundhay route followed in 1897 by one to Kirkstall Abbey, though its horse-tram service had originated in 1871. The forerunner of the present day juggernaut lorry was the steam traction engine which was developed towards the end of the century, effective in the heavy loads it was able to move from point to point but, like the trams, slow, noisy and dirty.

During the last twenty years or so cycling became popular for recreation and exercise as well as for the express purpose of an individual moving from place to place. The combination of poor shaking experience, but nevertheless many people were prepared to have a go. As early as 1869 there was a national cycle exhibition at Studley Royal; the Sheffield Bicycle Club was founded in the 1870s and on the 5th August, 1878, the Cycle Touring Club was founded in Harrogate by a medical student, Stanley Cotterell. Another method of 'transport' worthy of mention is the electric telegraph which came into public usage in 1870 and meant that for the first time the furthest parts of the country were linked for the quick transmission of messages.

At the end of Victoria's long reign in 1901, a period which had seen such remarkable progress in transport methods, the country was on the threshold of still more extraordinary advances; not only were the first motor cars appearing on the roads, but man was soon to take to the air by means of powered flight. The 19th century inaugurated an ease and speed of communications that shrank distances and offered a mobility unbelievable to any earlier generation.

6.   Leisure

THE VICTORIAN ERA witnessed a great leap forward in one particular aspect of leisure activity that is nowadays quite commonplace and virtually taken for granted, namely travel and the taking of holidays. The Napoleonic campaigns had remade the European map and were firing the enthusiasm of people to go and see for themselves. There was a growing interest and curiosity about the world, enhanced by poets, novelists and artists, which stimulated many to see parts of Great Britain away from their home areas as well as venture further afield to see for themselves the glories of the past in such countries as France and Italy. An annual holiday was becoming an indispensable part of family life—that is for those who could afford it. Coalfield populations went to the East Coast and those from the woollen areas to the West Coast.

The 19th century witnessed the widespread expansion of transport with the development of roads and railways and the change from sailing ships to vessels powered by steam. Men like. Telford and Macadam were transforming the face of the countryside, and at the same time law and order were getting the better of the footpad and highwayman so that ordinary men and women could go about their lawful occasions with a greater degree of comfort and safety than had previously been the case.

The ability to travel naturally depended on the financial circumstances of the family. Those in the poorest and meanest strata of society had to content themselves with a day out in the country at a place easy and cheaply of access from the industrial conurbations in the south and west of the county. Ilkley, Harrogate, Knaresborough, the Dales and the Dukeries were popular with the masses, though those with more time and money available would perhaps choose Scarborough, which could be considered the most fashionable of Yorkshire's resorts during this period. Others on the coast, however, were also developing and Redcar, Saltburn, Whitby, Filey and Bridlington each had their adherents. The cult of 'going on holiday' was developing rapidly and one of the first tourist guides was soon to be published by the enterprising firm of Black.

Those fortunate individuals who comprised the middle and

upper classes would possess their own conveyance, a horse-drawn waggonette or coach, by which they would be able to make their holiday, or even day out, into a tour, stopping off for refreshment or to admire the view or spend the night as they pleased. Those more ambitious, adventuresome and above all financially 'well-heeled' would desport themselves at the fashionable resorts on the continent or enjoy the intellectual delights of the Grand Tour. In the early years of the queen's reign it occurred to a certain Baptist missionary, Thomas Cook by name, that it would prove desirable, not to say profitable, to arrange organised tours in Britain in conjunction with the Midland Railway company. At the time of the Great Exhibition in 1851 a return trip to London would cost a citizen of Bradford or Leeds the princely sum of 5s. (25p). From such humble beginnings was the worldwide travel agency formed.

For those who journeyed to the coast the range of enjoyment would be somewhat limited by present day standards. The sea air was of course there to invigorate and refresh as was the sea itself. Bathing machines were an 18th century invention but were still very much in use a century later. Basically a covered four-wheeled cart, they were drawn into the sea by a horse between the shafts and when a convenient distance from the shore the lady or gentleman would descend into the water. After their bathe they would re-enter the machine to dress and return to the shore. The sexes were strictly segregated, this being achieved by the simple expedient of having different timing arrangements for ladies and gentlemen. Other attractions would be a pier, a parade, promenade or esplanade named according to its grandiosity or the sophistication of the resort, and possibly a theatre, library and assembly room. Popular events for a wet afternoon or evening would have been the pierrots, nigger minstrels or music hall held in all probability on the pier. For those of a somewhat more elevated frame of mind there may have been concerts given by a 'Palm Court Orchestra' or band.

Whit Monday walks allowed one to forget the harsher realities of the period. The summer holidays centred round the feast weeks when the mills would close down and the workers, provided they could afford the expense, would go away to Blackpool, Morecambe, Scarborough and other coastal resorts in Lancashire and Yorkshire. Those without the means to go away to stay resorted to a day out at Hardcastle Crags, Almscliff Crag, Shipley Glen, Bolton Abbey or even Ingleborough or Aysgarth Falls if they lived in the industrial north of the West Riding. For those living further south there were the Peak District and the Dukeries. It was fortunate that virtually all the industrial belt from Sheffield, Rotherham and Doncaster in the south to Bradford and Leeds in the north was easy of access to open-air outlets.

It was during the Victorian age that the development of spas as resorts really began to explode over most of the country and in this respect Ilkley and Harrogate were Yorkshire's representatives. First and foremost they had the advantage of being in beautiful countryside and yet were easy of access from the industrial areas. As holidays were short, frequently only a day's length for the less fortunate, this was an important point in their favour as was the fact that the expense of travelling to them was minimal. A working day for young and old alike would be up to 10½ hours in extent for six days of the week and it was only latterly that work on Saturdays was limited to the mornings, though the Bank Holiday Acts of 1871 and 1875 did allow a few extra days per year for leisure activities.

The waters of Harrogate had been used medicinally for over two hundred years before Victoria came to the throne but conditions for the patients were primitive in the extreme. There were several inns and hostelries but nothing in the way of what one might term 'superior accommodation', though there were at least three hotels in existence—the Crown, Dragon and Granby—and it was to these that the gentry gravitated. The accession of the young queen saw a dramatic advancement in the development of the town. Betty Lupton, a legendary figure, was 'Queen of the Wells'. For 50 years to 1845 she dispensed waters which came from an original spring, dipping into it with a long handled horn spoon and distributing sulphurous, evil smelling drink to regulars who rose early.

In 1841 an Act of Parliament made sweeping changes in the administration of the town, 21 commissioners being appointed. They were elected for a three year period, seven of them retiring annually and as a body they had wide powers, one of which was the protection of the mineral springs for which purpose they were empowered to make by-laws for their management. The commissioners must have taken their obligations seriously for by the following year they had erected the Royal Pump Room over the old sulphur well. This was followed in 1846 by the illumination of the streets by gas. In 1848 an Act of Parliament was obtained for the supplying of water and the first reservoirs were constructed at Harlow Hill followed in 1866 by one at Haverah Park. Two years later the town's sewerage scheme was completed. Thus in some 25 years great advances were made in the town's public utilities. Whilst all this was in progress, hotels, shops and religious establishments were being developed at a similar pace, but it was not until 1898 that the Royal Baths were opened by the Duke of Cambridge, one of the queen's sons.

The advent of the railway was also an important factor in the town's development as a spa, resort and residential area, bringing many manufacturers and merchants to live there whose places of business were Bradford, Leeds and the smaller industrial towns of the West Riding. In 1843 the Royal Mail and 14 other coaches maintained regular daily services passing through or to or from

Harrogate. Five years later the first rail link was forged, the station being erected where the Prince of Wales Hotel stood until recent times close to the junction of the Leeds and York roads on the Stray. Ten years later the system of communication was complete; a new station opened on the 2nd August, 1862, on its present site and the town left the age of the stage-coach and was thrust into the modern age of steam.

Ilkley was a small village until Victorian times. It was the arrival of the railway on the 1st August, 1865, from Bradford and Leeds, which was ultimately extended on the 1st October, 1888, to Skipton, that resulted in its growth as a dormitory town similar to Harrogate. The sixty years of the queen's reign coincided with the town's heyday as a hydropathic centre; two fine hydros were erected, one of which is the present College of Education. Formerly it was the Wells House Hotel designed in the Italianate style by Cuthbert Brodrick, who also was the architect of Leeds Town Hall. It was built in 1860, sixteen years later than the Scottish baronial style Ben Rhydding Hydro, a curious name derived from Bean Ridding, a bean field delineated on an old map. A village of the same name grew up round the hotel and a station was built especially to cater for the arrival and departure of the guests. The village has now been absorbed by Ilkley, the hotel demolished and the site occupied by private housing development. Ilkley's celebrations of the Golden Jubilee of the queen's reign were no doubt typical of many other townships in the county. There were massed choirs, bands, a procession, athletic sports, a greasy pole contest, presents for children and a tea for them and 250 old people. The day ended with a fireworks display. Houses and streets were appropriately decorated and the Ilkley Gas Light Company put on what we would now refer to as 'a commercial'. Minor or lost spas were to some extent still functioning in Yorkshire, e.g. Addingham, Barnsley, Malton, Ripon, Skipton, Slaithwaite, Tadcaster and Wakefield.

Leisure pursuits undertaken nearer home were in some degree of the same style as those of today—cricket, football, racing, bowls, archery and even croquet being popular. Quoits, skittles and knurr and spell were also favoured in some areas but these were very localised and only survive tenuously at the present time. One of the year's most popular sporting occasions in the county, the Scarborough Cricket Festival, was founded in 1871. Professionalism as it is known nowadays was virtually non-existent and so the accent was far more on participation than on watching. It was only towards the end of the century that people performed for money. Pigeon and whippet racing were practised in the industrial areas south of Leeds and in the city itself there was a bear pit in use from 1840 to 1868. Cock fighting, hare coursing, horse riding, fox hunting with beagles and shooting over dogs were practised in the rural areas, and skating and sledging, then as now, were pastimes enjoyed by young and old during the winter months.

Dancing classes and academies proliferated and in the early 1870s Bradford had its Belle Vue Rink in Manningham Lane for roller skating, followed twenty years later in the same vicinity by the Valley Parade Rink. The city had a swimming club formed in 1880, and the Dolphin Club founded in 1897 specialised in water-polo. Billiards and snooker were popular pastimes, frequently being played in coffee taverns, and the gentry practised the skills of archery, lawn tennis and cricket. The famous Park Avenue ground at Bradford was opened in July 1880, though the club had been formed 44 years earlier. The ground at one time offered a wide range of games; apart from cricket these included archery, lawn tennis, quoits, rugby and of course soccer, the first match of which was played on the 14th September, 1895. There was also a race track. Perhaps somewhat unlikely, two years before Park Avenue was opened, the city had a bicycle club.

Theatre visits were of course popular but were the prerogative of the more well to do as were musical performances given by well known artists and choirs. Many of the latter were formed during the Victorian era and are still flourishing to this day, though considerably more famous. One of these, the Huddersfield Choral Society, was founded in 1836; in the early days male members paid 5s. (25p.) per annum for the privilege of membership, though females were allowed free membership. There was a generous perk for members, however, for at each meeting they were granted 'three gills of ale and bread and cheese'. Practices were held monthly to coincide with the full moon for the benefit of members walking from a distance. Curiously, considering its present world-wide fame, the object of the Society in its earlier days was not public performance but merely enjoyable practice. Members took turns to choose the oratorio to be performed at the next meeting and each had the opportunity to express his or her opinion of the music after the performance provided it was done 'in a respectable, friendly and becoming manner'.

Bradford Choral Society is another organisation with a long history of success; if was founded in 1847 and within eleven years it had performed at the Crystal Palace and at Buckingham Palace in the presence of the queen and 'a select audience of 210 personages'. In October 1881, when the Town Hall was opened, it performed at a three day festival of music with the Halle Orchestra, Albani and Patti being the soloists. Twenty-seven years previously Charles Halle, founder of the famous orchestra, had made his first public appearance in the city as a solo pianist. Long before the Town Hall opened its doors a much more famous hall associated with music was in existence. St George's Hall celebrated its opening on 31st August, 1853, with a grand musical festival; 86 players were in the orchestra and there were eight soloists and a choir of 150 conducted by Mr Costa of the Royal Italian Opera. Another festival was staged three years later and a third in 1859. The Festival Choral Society at its inaugural concert in 1858 was fortunate to have Jenny Lind, Clara Howells and Sims Reeves as soloists; also a certain Mrs Sunderland, the ':Yorkshire Queen of Song', whose name is perpetuated in the Mrs Sunderland musical competitions. Not to be outdone by Bradford and Huddersfield, Leeds founded its own festival in 1858.

Lighter and more popular music was frequently performed in the local bandstand, that of Lister Park in Bradford being renowned for such concerts since 1871. Performances essentially were free of charge save only for a possible collection taken in a bag or box passed around the audience by well wishers of the performers. These concerts were almost always given by brass or silver bands which had their founding members among the work forces of the mills, factories and collieries. From humble beginnings such as this are the present day descendants, as instanced by the Black Dyke Mills Band of Queensbury founded in 1835. Many of these bands are now combinations of high quality professionalism, in demand all over the country and frequently performing under the direction of the finest conductors in the land.

The world of brass bands was originally localised in the heavy industrial areas of Yorkshire and Lancashire; there it had its roots and there it flourished, but now, thanks to radio, T.V. and recordings, it has spread far beyond the confines of its birth. Rural communities had to be satisfied with more rudimentary performances but even some of the smallest villages had their bands, most of them being formed during the last forty years of the century, and what the players lacked in expertise they more than made up in enthusiasm. Swaledale was particularly enterprising because Keld, Gunnerside, Reeth and Arkengarthdale all had bands, whilst that of Muker originated in 1897 in a burst of patriotism and loyalty to commemorate the queen's Diamond Jubilee. When Askrigg railway station was opened in 1877, Gunnerside band played a prominent part in the celebrations after arriving in a conveyance drawn by a dozen grey horses.

Theatres supplied a wide range of entertainment ranging from the culture and sophistication provided by the Alhambra in Bradford and The Grand in Leeds, which opened on 18th November, 1878, to the lighter fare of the music hall put on at such places as the City Varieties and Empire in Leeds. So popular was this form of entertainment that there were eight such establishments in Leeds and ten in Sheffield in 1868. Many famous performers visited Yorkshire to tread the boards of its theatres and music halls—Henry Irving, who died in Bradford shortly after appearing at the Alhambra in 1905, Henry Ainley, Sims Reeves,

Beerbohn Tree, George Arliss, Huntley Wright, Forbes Robertson, Matheson Lang, Gerald du Maurier, Ellen Tarry, Lily Langtry, Ada Reeve, Gertie Millar, Rosie Boote, Irene Vanburgh, Mrs. Patrick Campbell, Little Titch, Wilson Barrett, Frank Benson, Sarah Bernhardt, Maire Lloyd and Dan Leno. Christmas time entertainment was the pantomime and this was put on at both types of theatre which vied with each other to attract the whole family with a lavishness and glamour that did not count the cost. Prior to the coming of the music hall, singing rooms were popular and may be said to have been the forerunner of the variety theatres. They were usually attached to public houses, were rather bawdy affairs and attracted the less desirable element of society. Bradford seems to have made something of a speciality of this form of entertainment in Yorkshire, though on the credit side it also supported rather more theatres than might have been expected. The city had a Theatre Royal in Duke Street as early as 1844; twenty years later the Royal Alexandra opened in Manningham Lane, though it only retained the name for three years because it was then re-named the Theatre Royal when the original building of that name was closed. These were followed by the Palace in 1875, the Princes in 1876 whose opening attraction was the Carl Rosa Opera Co., and the Empire in 1899. The Palace had the unique honour of presenting the first cinematograph show in the city on 6th April, 1896.

Galas, feasts, circuses, carnivals and shows of various kinds were popular with the masses because they were cheap, being held practically on their own doorsteps, and bright, noisy and gay, bringing life and jollity to otherwise somewhat hard and desolate lives. Lee Gap Fair, near Morley, and Woodhouse and Holbeck Feasts at Leeds were probably the best known and would encompass all the usual excitement of roundabouts, helter skelter, swing boats, hoop-la, coconut shies, cake-walks, fortune telling, prize fighting and the exhibition of freaks. Pea and pie and brandy snap stalls would be there to assist the maintenance of strength and conviviality. Add all this to the bright lights and music of the steam organs and the scene was set for an enjoyable and happy evening.

Similar events in rural areas were of necessity less ambitious and took rather different forms. There were Punch and Judy shows, German dancing bears, racing, jumping, weight lifting and throwing, wrestling and the crudities of bare-fisted fighting. It is interesting to recall Grinton Feast and Sports held on 18-20th August, 1873, at which the following events took place. A pony and donkey race for the prize of a bridle, dog trails for a kettle, boys' races for caps, quoit playing for a teapot, jumping for gloves, pole-jumping for 3s. (15p), men's and boys' three-legged race for a hat, 200 yards race for 10s. (50p), a race with a first prize of 4s. (20p) and a second prize of 2s. (10p), and a waggoners' race for a whip. One cannot imagine the present generation waxing enthusiastic over such a prize list.

At Reeth, fairs were held on the Green, though these might properly be classified as markets. A useful adjunct was that seven public houses were open all day on such occasions. At Lothersdale the annual feast and sports were livened by the playing of the Carleton and Cowlingshaw brass bands. Allotment, agricultural, flower and horticultural shows and societies flourished generally all over the county and many well known ones were founded in this period, including that of Stokesley in 1859 and Egton Bridge thirty years later. One of the more unusual but certainly worthwhile societies was formed in 1884; the Cleveland Bay Horse Society has fortunately been instrumental in preserving the famous breed. Another pursuit of the countryside was Morris dancing, still keeping a tenuous hold on the past in a few areas of the Dales today. Also still surviving are two curiosities originating in Victorian times, one in an industrial area and the other in the countryside. The famous Denby Dale pie was first made in 1846 in celebration of the repeal of the Corn Laws and it was made again to commemorate the queen's Golden Jubilee in 1887. The White Horse at Kilburn was designed by schoolmaster Thomas Taylor who was helped by thirty local men to set it up on a sloping hillside above the village; covering an area of two acres and measuring 314 ft. from nose to tail and 228 ft. from hoof to shoulder—it was completed in 1857. Visits to spectacular pieces of scenery were also popular: for instance, Malham Cove and Bempton Cliffs. The latter's desecration was prevented by an Act of Parliament promoted by Sir Christopher Sykes in 1869.

Of all forms of entertainment, Victoria's reign has become synonymous with that provided in the home. Domestic based pastimes were popular because not only were they inexpensive but invariably involved the whole family with singing, instrument playing—usually of the piano or violin, charades, cards and other games and impromptu dancing if space permitted. The singing of ballads round the piano and fireside is probably most people's image of Victorian home life and it has been well preserved in prose, verse, music and visual arts.

No mention of the home can pass without reference to the children. Those born into working class families led lives fundamentally not very different from their parents. There was the minimum of education and many a child worked long hours in the factories and mills, some from as young as eight years old. Open spaces and playing fields were practically non-existent in the industrial towns, certainly until late in the century when matters did improve with the more enlightened local authorities either purchasing or acquiring by gift open spaces which are today still appreciated and enjoyed. Leeds City Council purchased Roundhay Park in 1872 for

£139,000, a lot of money in those days but surely a bargain if ever there was one when viewed in the perspective of a hundred years of pleasure enjoyed by countless thousands of young and old alike. Another acquisition of note was the gift to the city by Col. North in 1890 of Kirkstall Abbey, not only an outstanding historical monument but an additional lung for the citizens. Bradford was equally enterprising, Peel Park being acquired by the Corporation in 1863, Lister Park in 1870 for the sum of £40,000 from Lord Masham and Horton Park for £42,000 in 1873. In spite of these public spaces where such things as swings and seesaws were erected, children who did not live reasonably close to these amenities had no alternative to playing in the drab and dingy streets near their homes. Probably the only bright spot in their young lives was the occasional Sunday School treat or outing which might entail a day out in the country with a picnic thrown in for good measure.

Children living in country districts would have led better lives than their town dwelling cousins since, although their parents would be equally hard pressed financially and worked long hours on the land and in rural industries, at least they had fresh air and open spaces in which to play and relax. Children of both town and country would have to be content with games and toys of the simplest kind and, by present day standards, decidedly unsophisticated. Whip and top, shuttlecock and battledore, stilts, skipping, hopscotch, diabolo and marbles—commonly referred to as taws— were popular, as were football and cricket played with home made equipment. Swimming would be enjoyed by those within access of a river or canal unpolluted by industrial effluent.

As the reign progressed more and more public buildings were erected and brought into use for those of the population who wished to broaden their intellectual capacity in what spare time was available. University education commenced; for example, the Victoria University College at Leeds dated from 1874. Mechanics Institutes sprang up all over the country and these provided meeting places, particularly for the less well to do, to socialise and participate in activities not really possible before—activities such as dancing, gymnastics and music making. The Institutes were also used to house the new free libraries which were established in 1850-51 and were popular with those who could read. Separate buildings to house these were somewhat slow to develop and it was not until 1872 that Bradford's reference library and reading rooms were opened, followed a year later by the lending library. Parallel development was simultaneously taking place in other towns and cities coupled with the establishment of art galleries and museums, that at Leeds for example being opened in 1888. These were instrumental in allowing the visual arts to be appreciated by the man in the street who would have had little or no opportunity of visiting the great collections in London. Evening classes were also instigated in the Mechanics Institutes and were a great help to those who were prepared to make the effort to fit themselves for more responsible duties at their places of work. By late century, as traffic and tram lines pushed old fairs out of the main streets, Temperance and Friendly Societies organised galas for fund raising, while local newspapers made the working classes avid readers and dialect literature was undertaken by many inspired factory workers.

Primarily, leisure made people forget the daily drudgery of work in mills and factories.

7. Personalities

YORKSHIRE provided personalities from every facet of life during the Victorian era and they all contributed in their varied ways to the prosperity of the county. In the nineteenth century they were eminent for talent and rich endowment of the qualities of a particular character of Yorkshire folk—energy, resourcefulness and perseverance. Many of the most famous Yorkshiremen of modern times, while retaining essential Yorkshire characteristics, carried talents out of the county and were so celebrated in other spheres that their origin was lost. Surprisingly few of the Yorkshiremen remained in the county all their lives.

Nearly every great Yorkshire town has had at some time or other a particular man who helped above all others to build its fortunes. Yorkshiremen were to the fore on the episcopal bench of the established Church and in statesmanship and politics Yorkshire's reputation was also prominent—for instance Roebuck advocated radicalism before it came to be as evident as is now commonplace.

The themes of writers fell into two groups—those connected with industrial, domestic and working conditions and those sentimentalising country life as an idyllic state of existence, far removed from the townsfolks' conditions. Humorous poems were composed by nineteenth century poets, some of which had a satirical vein, for example 'pedantic schoolmasters and prudish parsons'. It is from such writings and those of personalities and local historians, as well as parish registers, that a picture of Victorian Yorkshire can be gleaned. Personalities had to contend with the social movements of the Industrial Revolution and their tempo rose and fell with the mood of the age. Famous people characterised the development of social activities in the Victorian age and brought all walks together in a self conscious mingling. Many made their stamp on life in an era when initiative and innovation were essential if Victorian Yorkshire was to prosper.

With the rapid increase in technology as a result of the Industrial Revolution, it was necessary to deal with the growing social problems associated with the industrial changes. Few were willing to take on such a task, but one such person was Sir Titus Salt—born at Morley in September 1803—who became a well known manufacturer and philanthropist. In 1822, his family moved to Bradford where his father started a business as a wool stapler. He was joined by Titus who attended the wool sales in London and Liverpool and bought wool from the farmers in East Anglia and Lincolnshire. Titus, having achieved knowledge working for his father, launched out on his own, spinning and weaving the wool into fabric. Soon he was carrying on business in four mills in various parts of Bradford, specialising in alpaca and mohair products for which he was awarded a medal at the Great Exhibition in 1851. He began to take an active part in the affairs of the city becoming an alderman and in 1848 its second mayor. In 1859 he became the Liberal member for Bradford but because of ill health resigned two years later, and then years later he was created a baronet. In 1850 he decided to bring together into one area his plant, machinery and work force, and to this end purchased a site at Saltaire. Building went on apace and during the next twenty years as described in an earlier chapter, the site became a township in its own right, with amenities adjunct to civilised living. Nearby there was established a 14 acre park with boating, swimming and games facilities. In an age when the lot of the working class left very much to be desired, the establishment of Saltaire was an astonishing advance in social and industrial progress. Bradford was also the recipient of Salt's generosity, receiving over the years donations towards the building of hospitals, churches, orphanages and the founding of grammar school scholarships. Charities also benefited and he even gave a lifeboat to Stornoway. He died at his home in Lightcliffe in December 1876.

Richard Oastler was as equally concerned with the plight of the labouring classes as Salt. He was born at Leeds in 1789 and died in Harrogate in 1861, and might have lived the last thirty years of his life in as much obscurity as the first forty if, as is so often the case, a chance encounter had not sparked off a latent reforming zeal. Richard's father, Robert, was a cloth merchant in Leeds and was a man of some substance. He sent the youngest of his eight children to the Moravian boarding school at Fulneck, which no doubt played a considerable part in moulding the character of the boy for his future welfare work. On leaving school, he followed his father into the cloth trade and soon got involved with philanthropists in assisting the less fortunates in life. Unfortunately his business went bankrupt, but luckily Richard was able to step into his father's shoes on Robert's death in 1820. After a period as a landowner's steward, a chance encounter occurred with a worsted spinner, John Wood, who recounted to an incredulous Richard the plight of children working in the city's mills. From that time onwards, Richard devoted his life to mitigating the appalling conditions which existed as a result of the Industrial Revolution in respect of men, women and children. Newspaper and parliamentary campaigns were organised as well as workers' rallies and marches. Philanthropists supported him and the future Lord Salisbury was a notable ally—it was largely due to him that abuses were brought before Parliament. Oastler was of impetuous disposition and became angry and embittered when the reforms he so long desired were blocked or frustrated by irate mill owners and parliamentary debate and procedures. Wood withdrew from his association when Oastler publicly advocated sabotage in the mills as a method of achieving his objectives more speedily. Worse was to follow as he was sued for debt and his health broke down. The debt was proved and Oastler was committed to prison to serve a sentence of three years and two months.

Prior to conviction he had twice unsuccessfully contested by-elections at Huddersfield, it being safe to say that his failure was due entirely to the working class with whom he was so popular not having the vote. In Fleet Prison he devoted himself entirely to writing the Fleet Papers. These set out his advocacy for the reform of society and social progress, and when he was released from prison and returned to his native county he got a rapturous welcome from those whose welfare he had so much at heart. There is no doubt that he was one of the pioneers of social justice and reform as we know them today and the instigator of measures that would ultimately do away with the worst of the evils that afflicted those who worked in mills and factories. He was also one of the instigators of factory reform which has led to the enlightened conditions that now prevail in our industrial cities and towns. One of Oastler's admirers, Michael Sadler, a scholar and educationalist, born in Barnsley in 1861, was concerned at the lack of secondary education and poor opportunities for the working classes, and his agitation led to the 1902 Act.

A man concerned with child welfare, Benjamin Waugh, born in Settle in 1839, started the London Society for Prevention of Cruelty to Children, which was the foundation of the N.S.P.C.C. Seebohm Rowntree, the industrial philanthropist (like Salt) and sociologist, was also concerned at the social aspects of the Industrial Revolution. He was born in York in 1871, and starting in the 1890s devoted a large part of his life to the betterment of living conditions of the poorer members of society of which he was not a member.

Philip Snowden, born at Cowling in 1864, like Rowntree was deeply influenced by his parents and their enlightened attitude to the problems of the age. Snowden's parents were poor mill workers whose political views were radical and who were staunch Methodists. After initial work in an insurance office, Philip moved to the Inland Revenue and began a study of socialism from books and pamphlets. When Keir Hardie founded the Independent Labour Party at Bradford in 1893, Philip became one of its earliest adherents. He started to make political speeches and write on social and political subjects for newspapers and journals, and by the time of Victoria's death he was within two years of becoming chairman of the Independent Labour Party.

One of Snowden's later political opponents was the Liberal politician, Herbert Asquith, born at Morley in 1852. After a brilliant academic career he was obviously destined for notable achievements in whatever course in life he chose to follow. After qualifying in law at Lincolns Inn, he stood for Parliament and was elected for East Fife in 1886. Within six years he had been appointed Home Secretary by Gladstone when the Liberals were returned to power in 1892. The Government was defeated three years later but in that short period of office Asquith saw the Factory Bill onto the Statute Book, a measure which was directed to the betterment of the safety and health of working people. Ironically, in 1893 he was accused of victimising workpeople only a few miles from his birthplace when, as a result of rioting caused by a coal strike at Featherstone, troops were called out by the local authority to quell the disturbance and two of the demonstrators were shot dead.

Apart from the social aspects of the Industrial Revolution, the transport aspects also received attention. Thus George Hudson, born at Howsham in 1801, achieved notoriety as 'the railway king'. Initially he was an apprentice to a linen draper. He moved into a large house in Monkgate to entertain on a lavish scale and interested himself in public affairs, becoming Lord Mayor of York in 1837. He had a flair for railways and possessed far-seeing vision regarding transport. He tried to persuade George Stephenson to make York a key junction but Stephenson refused. Hudson got a Parliamentary Bill passed allowing him to construct a line from York to Normanton, and in 1839 the York and Midland Railway company ran the first train over this route from York, where the station was a wooden building with one clerk and manager. Hudson visualised connecting York with London and Edinburgh and also built lines to Whitby and Scarborough which were developed as pleasure resorts. In spite of opposition virtually all he attempted succeeded. He became known as 'the railway king' and every railway board sought his services as chairman. He became M.P. for Sunderland and had a special train built; with 500 citizens he rode there in style. He bought two Yorkshire estates—Newby Park and Londesborough, for £½ million. He built his own private station at the latter after the line to Market Weighton had been constructed. His head was turned by success and numerous railway companies were created. The country went railway mad and avidly bought up shares, while a finance house was created in London. In 1848, 23 years before his death, Hudson's world crashed around him, with revelations of manipulated accounts.

Far removed from the trials and tribulations of the Industrial Revolution were photographers, musicians and painters. The Kearton brothers, born and brought up in a remote part of Swaledale, were destined to become the founders and popularisers of natural history by their writings and photography on the subject. It is true to say that they were the ancestors of all those enthusiasts, both amateurs and professionals, who contribute to the prolific output of books, magazines, radio and T.V. programmes which have done so much to fascinate and interest a large percentage of the population and to make people more aware of their natural heritage. Both brothers were born at Thwaite—Richard in 1862 and Cherry in 1871. Richard was the first person to popularise natural history in Britain by lecturing and writing in non-scientific language which the ordinary man could understand and identify. Cherry likewise was the first to illustrate books on natural history with photographs and the first to go out into the wild to film big game. Thus, by combining their talents they formed a formidable team of all round ability to portray their chosen subject to an ever widening public. For some years they were associated with the publishing firm of Cassell in London, but towards the end of the century they left to freelance and become full-time naturalists and to travel the world. Another naturalist at this time—concentrating on ornithology and writing—was 'Squire' Waterton, born at Wakefield, who established the first known bird sanctuary in South America in the 1840s and wrote about his experience.

The composer Frederick Delius was born at Bradford on 29 January, 1862. He was educated at the Grammar School and all his life enjoyed the wide open spaces. In his youth he spent holidays at Filey, enjoyed the Scarborough Cricket Festivals and delighted in riding his pony over Rombalds Moor to appreciate the beauty of Wharfedale. Nearly all his works were inspired by nature and to them he applied evocative titles of the great outdoors. He was influenced by Grieg and Debussy but the impressionistic unfamiliar idiom of his music won little acclaim from Victorian critics and audiences. He travelled widely in Europe and from 1889 he settled in France, until his death in 1934.

Sir Edward Bairstow, another Yorkshire born composer, originated from Huddersfield in 1879. By the end of the century he had served his articles at Westminster Abbey and was organist at Leeds Parish Church. Bacchus Dykes, a hymn writer/composer and contributor to 'Hymns Ancient & Modern', was born in Hull in 1823. He composed 55 hymn tunes before his death in 1876, including 'Holy, Holy, Holy Lord God Almighty', 'Praise to the Holiest', 'King of Love my Shepherd is', 'Eternal Father' and 'Lead Kindly Light'. Sir Walter Parratt, born at Huddersfield in 1841, was an organist and composer who became Master of the Queen's Music and Professor of Music at Oxford. Wakefield produced Keith Leighton who composed works for piano, string quartets, concertos for violin, piano and cello and choral works.

Mrs. Sunderland, a leading North of England soprano, was born in 1819, and engaged to sing at choral concerts in Buckingham Palace. She perhaps sung in many choral works composed by Sir William Sterndale Bennett, who was born in Sheffield in 1816 and died in 1875. He held important posts in the music world, including permanent conductor of the Philharmonic Society concerts, Professor of Music at Cambridge and Principal of the Royal Academy of Music. He also composed overtures and symphonies.

Sir John Etty, the York born painter of historical subjects, a colourist and untiring student of the living figure, was a rival of Constable. His landscapes and drapery always harmonised admirably with his figures, though his almost exclusive speciality was the nude, of which he made extremely faithful studies, often in the representation of mythological characters. Etty helped to found a school of design in York, the first of its kind in the provinces, and his last three large pictures in the 1840s were on the theme of Joan of Arc. On his death in 1848 he left 30 unfinished paintings, 60 Old Masters and two suits of armour. A younger contemporary of Etty was Sir William Frith, born near Ripon, an associate of the Royal Academy in 1845. In 1853 his painting of Ramsgate led to an exhibition that year at the Academy, after which 'Ramsgate Sands' joined the Royal Collection. Frederick Leighton, born in Scarborough in 1830, was also associated with the Royal Academy being its President in 1878—he was the first painter to be given a peerage.

Also in the field of arts, regional novelists gave to the Yorkshire countryside an enhanced topography. The Brontë family were pre-eminent, yet Branwell and his sisters, Charlotte, Emily and Anne, wrote most of their works before Victoria came to the throne. They were attached to the parsonage and the other freedom hinterland, the moors, where they renewed strength. Charlotte wrote 'The Professor', 'Jane Eyre', 'Shirley' and 'Villette', while Emily prepared 'Wuthering Heights' and Anne 'Agnes Grey' and the 'Tenant of Wildfell Hall'.

Lesser known writers included George Gissing (1857-1903), born in Wakefield—a genius wasted and a good class scholar and novel writer who worked on the 'Private Papers of H. Rycroft'. Poets have included Alfred Austin, Poet Laureate, born in Leeds in 1835, and Sir William Watson, born in 1858 in Burley-in-Wharfedale. Gertie Millar, the famous actress born in Bradford in 1879, played in 'Babes in the Wood' pantomime in 1892 at Manchester and in 1900 in Bradford.

Closely related to the writing fraternity were such people as philologists and lexicographers. An example was Joseph Wright, born in Thackley in 1855, who could neither read nor write until the age of 17, yet he took a PhD at Heidelberg and Corpus Christi and was Professor of Comparative Philology at Oxford at the age of 36. He studied old languages and wrote their grammars. From 1888 he taught Old High German at Oxford and worked on a Dialect Dictionary over 19 years, together with 14 primers and grammars.

Another high flying academic was William Stubbs, born in Knaresborough in 1825, who died in Oxford in 1901. In 1858 his 'Registrum Sacrum Anglicanum' exhibited the episcopal succession in England, and twelve years later he edited the Rolls Series of Select Charters. From 1884-8 he was Bishop of Chester and then went to Oxford. In 1871 he wrote a Constitutional History covering the period up to Tudor times. His specialist period was the twelfth century and his Rolls Series of prefaces introduces us to the chronicles, memorials and historical collections. A fellow cleric was Dean Inge, born in 1860 at Crayke—a powerful thinker who failed as a schoolmaster to keep order. He then tutored at Oxford on neo Platonic Mysticism and later in 1902 returned to theology. He later became Dean of St. Paul's Cathedral. Other Yorkshire scholars included Adam Sedgwick, born in Dent and Woodwardian Professor of Geology at Cambridge; James Tate, a gifted teacher and head of Richmond Grammar School; and Mark Pattison, a Rector of Lincoln College, Oxford.

Climbers and inventors can be classed as more intrepid characters willing to take risks. Cecil Slingsby, one of the first Alpine climbers, was born at Gargrave in 1849 and undertook many Alpine ascents from 1878 to 1902. He was the father of Norwegian mountaineering, who pioneered icemanship and rock climbing and was pro skiing. One of Yorkshire's more famous inventors was Sir George Cayley, born at Scarborough in 1773 and dying at Brompton in 1857. From 1831 to 1847, horrified by disasters on the railways, he wrote seven papers making suggestions for safety precautions, based on the belief that the human factor must be eliminated through fog signals and separate tracks for trains travelling in opposite directions. He also wrote on optics, electricity, acoustics and artificial limbs. He studied drainage and had agricultural allotments on his Brompton estates. In 1838 he became an associate of the Institution of Civil Engineers and five years later in a Mechanics Magazine he described an invention or convertiplane—four chopper screws for vertical lift, which closed to become wings with propellors for forward propulsion. In 1849 he constructed a second model glider and improved this in 1852 with a large glider in which his coachman flew across Brompton, an event that so scared him that he handed in his notice!

It was more down to earth developments, however, which made the Industrial Revolution. Harold Sorby of Sheffield, born in 1826, was the founder of metallography (the structure of metals)—now a developed technical science. He was a brilliant amateur in many fields and specialised in the application of natural science. Harry Brearley, the inventor of stainless steel, also born in the city, worked in the steelworks from childhood and was a writer of books on steel. He above all succeeded in producing an alloy of iron and chromium that would resist rust. Joseph Gillot of Sheffield became a steel pen-nib maker in Birmingham and Sir John Brown a naval vessel manufacturer.

Thus, Yorkshire in the 63½ years of Victoria's reign, produced a veritable gallery of important people—industrialists, social reformers, writers, philanthropists, musicians, artists, academics, clerics and lexicographers.

Bibliography

Barker, M. **Yorkshire North Riding** (London, 1976).

Bolton, D. **Yorkshire Revealed** (London, 1955).

Craven, A.B. **Victorian and Edwardian Yorkshire** (London, 1971).

Dewhirst, I. **Gleanings from Victorian Yorkshire** (Driffield, 1970).

Dewhirst, I. **Yorkshire Through the Years** (London, 1975).

Fairfax-Blakeborough, J. **Spirit of Yorkshire** (London, 1953).

Fieldhouse, J. **History of Bradford** (Longmans 1972; revised paperback edition, 1978).

Fletcher, J.S. **History of Yorkshire,** Vols. I to III (London, 1899-1901).

Fletcher, J.S. **Making of Modern Yorkshire 1750-1914** (London, 1918).

Fletcher, J.S. **Our Yorkshire** (London, 1899).

Grant, A. **Yorkshire** (London, 1975).

Hartley, M and Ingilby, J. **Life and Tradition in West Yorkshire** (London, 1968).

Hartley, M and Ingilby, J. **Yorkshire Dales** (London, 1968).

Hartley, M and Ingilby, J. **Yorkshire Portraits** (London, 1962).

Hattersley, R. **Goodbye to Yorkshire** (London, 1976).

Jackson, R. **Handbook for Tourists to Yorkshire** (Leeds, 1891).

Jones, G.R.J. (Ed). **Leeds and its Region** (Leeds, 1967).

Kitson-Clark, G. **Victorian England** (London, 1967).

Mayhall, J. **Annals of Yorkshire** Vols. I to III (Leeds, 1874).

Mee, A. (Ed). **Yorkshire West Riding** (London, 1941 and 1959).

Pevsner, N. **Buildings of England: Yorkshire West Riding** (London, 1959).

Raistrick, A. **Industrial Archeology** (London, 1972).

Scott, H. **Portrait of Yorkshire** (London, 1965).

Scott, H. **View of Yorkshire** (London, 1975).

Scott, H. **Yorkshire Heritage** (London, 1973).

Singleton, F.B. and Tate, W.E.   **History of Yorkshire** (London, 1965).

Singleton, F.B.   **Industrial Revolution in Yorkshire** (Dalesman, 1970).

Victoria County History of Yorkshire, Vols. I to III (reprinted, 1973-5).

Waddington-Feather, J.   **Leeds: The Heart of Yorkshire** (Leeds, 1967).

Walton, M.   **Sheffield: Its Story and Achievements** (Sheffield, 1968).

Wood, G.B.   **Historic Homes of Yorkshire** (London, 1957).

Young, G.M.   **Early Victorian England 1830-65** Vols. I and II (London, 1951 and 1954).

Young, G.M.   **Victorian England: Portrait of an Age** (London, 1960).